STUDIES IN THE UK ECONOMY

Multinationals

Richard Crum and Stephen Davies
University of East Anglia

Series Editor
Bryan Hurl
Head of Economics, Harrow School

HEINEMANN
EDUCATIONAL

Heinemann Educational,
a division of Heinemann Educational Books Ltd.
Halley Court, Jordan Hill, Oxford OX2 8EJ

OXFORD LONDON EDINBURGH
MADRID ATHENS BOLOGNA PARIS
MELBOURNE SYDNEY AUCKLAND SINGAPORE TOKYO
IBADAN NAIROBI GABORONE
PORTSMOUTH (NH) USA

© Richard Crum and Stephen Davies 1991

First published 1991
Reprinted 1995

British Library Cataloguing in Publication Data
Davies, Steve
    Multinationals. - (Studies in the UK economy).
    1. British multinational companies
    I. Title II. Crum, Richard III. Series 338.88941

ISBN 0-435-33011-X

Typeset and illustrated by Visual Image, Street.
Printed and bound in Great Britain by
Athenæum Press Ltd, Gateshead, Tyne & Wear

Acknowledgements

Thanks are due to the following for permission to reproduce copyright material:

Aquisitions Monthly for the tables on p.7; Associated Examining Board for question 3 on p.42; Chapman and Hall and Steve Globerman for the article on p.68 which appeared in *Applied Economics* 1979; the *Economist* for the article on pp.79–80; the *Financial Times* for the article on pp.25–6, the article on pp.43–4 by Paul Abrahams, the article on p.83 by William Dullforce and Martin Dickson, the article on p.84 by David Marsh, the article on p.87, and the article on p.90 by Guy de Jonquieres; Reproduced with the permission of Her Majesty's Stationery Office: the table on p.49 which appeared in *Economic Trends* 1990, the table on p.61 which appeared in *Census of Industrial Production* 1990, and the table on p.67 which appeared in *Census of Production* 1987; the *Independent* for the article on pp.34–5 by David Bowen; Joint Matriculation Board for question 4 on p.24; *Lloyds Bank Economic Bulletin* for the article on p.28, the table on p.46, and the chart on p.58; Oxford and Cambridge Examinations Syndicate for question 4 on p.78; the *Sunday Times* for the map on p.14 by Nick Kochan; Times Books Ltd for the table on p.3; Times Newspapers Ltd for the article on p.76 by Derek Harris; P.M. Townroe for the tables on pp.36–7, 38–9; The United Nations Centre of Transnational Corporations for the table on p.48; University of Cambridge Local Examinationbs Syndicate for question 4 on p.66; University of Oxford Delegacy of Local Examinations for question 5 on p.24, and question 3 on p.78; Unwin Hyman Ltd for the source material on pp.43-4 by John Dunning; Peter Williamson for the article on p.27 which appeared in the *Times*;

The Publishers have made every effort to contact the correct copyright holders. However, if any material has been incorrectly acknowledged we would be pleased to make the necessary arrangements at the earliest opportunity.

Contents

Preface

Textbooks cannot continue to ignore multinationals. On the macroeconomic front a well-known economist, Sir Alan Walters, using them as an economic indicator, writes:

'Last week's batch of statistics showed retail sales and industrial output falling. Most multinationals everywhere are reporting a slide in profits.'

Microeconomic theory, as the authors point out, is based on 'single-plant, single-product minnows' whereas the real world now, in manu-facturing, is dominated by 'multiplant, multiproduct, and multi-national giants' which call into question the degree to which teaching and learning in sixth forms is balanced and realistic. Governments, we are told, usually fall over backwards to attract multinationals to green-field sites, as inward foreign investment. But takeovers of domestic firms by foreign giants arouses xenophobic cries for protectionism. Is the first justified on economic grounds and the second not? The authors of this volume are experts on the subject, and the revelations of their research work are very exciting, pitched as they are at a level that is very approachable in schools because one of the authors is an A-level chief examiner.

Bryan Hurl
Series Editor

Chapter One
The nature and importance of multinational firms

'*Foseco Plc is the ultimate holding company of an industrial group whose principal business is speciality chemicals. The group has established over 100 operating companies in 36 countries.*'
Annual Report of Foseco Plc, 1989

Introduction

One of the major developments in the world economy in the second part of the twentieth century has been the expansion and proliferation of **multinational companies,** or as they are more usually labelled, **multinational enterprises** (often abbreviated in this book as MNEs).

In this chapter we shall provide an introductory discussion of the nature of these firms and why they are worthy of particular attention by economists. But first we need a clear definition. While the general meaning of the term multinational is obvious enough, it is open to various interpretations. The one adopted by most economists, and used throughout this book, is that an *MNE is a firm with production capacity located in more than one (and often many more than one) country*; such as Foseco Plc mentioned above. But by this definition we shall not be concerned, for example, either with firms merely exporting to other countries, or with financial companies investing in properties overseas. Needless to say, these other forms of international behaviour are both interesting and important, but the questions they raise are rather different.

MNEs already account for a large part of economic activity in most countries in the world, and it has been estimated that the 200 very largest of these firms have combined sales equivalent to about one-third of the gross domestic product (GDP) of the entire world. Moreover, it is a fairly safe bet to predict that in the next century their importance will grow still further with a tendency to the globalization of many industries.

Multinationals are especially important to the United Kingdom. Just as we were, and still are, one of the world's leading trading nations, so too UK firms were amongst the first to operate their production on an international scale. Indeed, many household name firms became multina-

1

tional even before the second part of this century. Even in recent years the UK remains second only to the USA in the scale of overseas operations of its firms. As can be seen from Table 1, virtually all our leading industrial firms operate overseas. Perhaps more surprisingly, even a large number of relatively smaller, less well known, UK firms have significant overseas operations: Foseco cited in the chapter head and the two firms considered in the following section are examples.

Nor is this a one-way phenomenon. Not only is the UK an important source (i.e. **home country**) of multinational firms, it also appears as an attractive location (i.e **host country**) for the operations of foreign companies. Again, it ranks second only behind the USA in the amount of investment it attracts from overseas multinational firms. Leading foreign-owned multinationals with significant operations in this country include: Ford, Peugeot, Esso, Texaco, Ciba-Geigy, Michelin, Nestlé, Shell, Nissan, Sanyo.

Some idea of the importance of multinationals, both UK and foreign-owned, to the British economy is revealed by the data in the table which charts the size and nature of the 20 largest industrial companies. It is interesting to note that the only firms we have marked as not having significant multinational operations are either nationalized (or only recently privatized) or in retail distribution. The former group is not surprising since nationalized firms were not encouraged to invest overseas. The latter group is less readily explainable, although you might like to reconsider why this is in the light of the theoretical discussion in the following chapter. In any event, it will be interesting to see whether these firms do 'go multinational' by the turn of the century.

Some case studies
As we have implied, it is not difficult to find examples of MNEs – they are all round us in everyday life. The examples on pages 4 and 5 have been chosen not because the firms concerned are necessarily large, but because, taken together, they illustrate some of the issues which will unfold in later chapters. A careful reading will reveal some common features, but also some interesting differences between the firms.

Table 1 The 20 largest industrial companies in the UK

Rank	Name	Activity (£million)	Turnover	Ownership*
1.	British Petroleum	Oil	33,101	UK MNE
2.	'Shell' Transport & Trading	Oil	22,329	UK MNE
3.	ICI	Petrochemicals, pharmaceuticals etc.	11,699	UK MNE
4.	Electricity Council	Electricity supply	11,366	NAT (recently privatized)
5.	BAT Industries	Tobacco, retailing, paper, financial services	11,358	UK MNE
6.	British Telecom	Telecommunication services	11,071	NAT (recently privatized)
7.	Hanson	Consumer products etc.	7,396	UK MNE
8.	British Gas	Gas supplies etc.	7,364	NAT (recently privatized)
9.	Shell UK	Oil	6,580	HOLL MNE
10.	Unilever	Food products, detergents, etc.	6,384	UK/HOLL MNE
11.	Grand Metropolitan	Hotel proprietors, milk products, brewers etc.	6,028	UK MNE
12.	Ford Motor Co.	Motor vehicles	5,936	USA MNE
13.	Esso UK	Oil industry	5,765	USA MNE
14.	J. Sainsbury	Retail distribution of food	5,659	UK Retail
15.	British Aerospace	Manufacture of aircraft	5,639	UK MNE
16.	General Electric Co.	Electrical engineers etc.	5,552	UK MNE
17.	BTR	Construction, energy & electrical etc.	5,472	UK MNE
18.	Gateway Corporation	Wholesale, retail	5,144	UK Retail
19.	Marks & Spencer	General stores	5,121	UK Retail
20.	British Steel	Manufacture of steel	4,906	UK MNE

* UK MNE indicates a UK firm with a significant proportion of its turnover generated by overseas operations. HOLL and USA indicate Dutch and US ownership. NAT indicates a nationalized, or only recently privatized, corporation. UK Retail indicates a UK firm engaged in retailing.

Source: *The Times 1000, 1989–1990* (Times Books Ltd, 1989)

Cadbury Schweppes PLC

Origins
Cadbury was established in 1824, selling chocolates as a sideline to tea and coffee. In 1969 it merged with Schweppes (established in 1897).

Multinational history
Cadbury acquired cocoa estates in Trinidad in 1897, and in 1920 began manufacture of confectionery in Australia. (Schweppes set up first overseas factory in Australia in 1870.)

Current status
Largest British-owned confectionery and soft drinks company. Products sold in 110 countries; production capacity in about 20 countries. Approximate world turnover: £3000 million; world employment: 35,000.

Product profile		*Country profile*	
Confectionery	40%	UK	45%
Beverages (soft drinks)	60%	Rest of Europe	20%
		North America	10%
		Australia & Others	25%

About 50 years after formation Cadbury began to export, mainly to Australia but also to South Africa and India. Then, in the early part of this century, it went multinational by producing in Australia and other old Empire countries. For this reason we might label the firm as having a 'Colonial' history. Especially following its merger with Schweppes in the 1960s, its operations spread rapidly around the world, notably to Europe and the USA. Recently very active in takeovers, it has acquired other leading British sweetmakers, Bassetts and Trebor. Recent overseas acquisitions have led to important market shares in many soft drinks markets in Europe and North America. It is also the joint owner (with the US multinational, Coca Cola) of the firm which manufactures all Schweppes and Coca Cola brands in the UK.

Sources: British Multinationals: Origins, Management and Performance, ed. Jones, G., Gower House, 1986, and Company Reports of Cadbury Schweppes

Bowater Industries PLC

Origins
Established in 1881 as paper merchants. Opened first paper mill (newsprint) in 1926.

Multinational history
First acquisitions overseas in Scandinavia in 1937. Over following 30–40 years opened greenfield mills and acquired local firms in many countries, notably USA, Canada and France.

Current status
Recent years have seen a changed focus. It has diversified out of its traditional

product, newsprint (the paper on which newspapers are printed), into the product range shown below. However, some of these products remain loosely connected with its roots in paper, although plastics have become increasingly more important. Approximate world turnover: £1300 million; world employment: 16,000.

Product profile		Country profile	
Printing/packaging	40%	Europe (mainly UK)	55%
Coating and laminates	10%	Australia	25%
Building materials	30%	North America	15%
Tissue & timber	10%	Others	5%
Engineering & others	10%		

Bowater was traditionally associated with newsprint, and at its peak it produced 10 per cent of the world's output. In the middle part of this century its expansion overseas was dramatic, being partly horizontal (i.e. producing newsprint in other countries), partly vertical (i.e. for the supplies of wood with which to produce paper) and partly integrated (i.e. both). But owing to a static market, it gradually diversified away into increasingly unrelated product areas, including double glazing and builders' merchants.

Source: *Bowater: A History*, Reader, W.J., Cambridge University Press, 1981

Three foreign multinationals in the UK

Ford (USA) is the second largest manufacturer of cars and trucks in the world. It is also a major producer of tractors, glass and steel. It has production facilities in about 100 countries, notably the USA, Canada, West Germany, Belgium and the UK. Its founder, Henry Ford, made and sold his first car in 1903. Expansion into the UK followed soon after, with Ford cars being assembled here in 1911. The British Ford Co. was formed in 1928, and Ford has had an important presence here ever since. It is now the largest car producer in the UK, employing over 40,000 workers (which is, nevertheless, only a small part of Ford's worldwide operations).

Heinz (USA) is one of the world's largest food manufacturers. It started producing horseradish in 1869 and was incorporated as a company in 1900. It quickly expanded its range of products (the original 57 varieties) and its operations overseas. From early this century its UK operations were an important part of the company. Currently it produces in 10 countries, with 40 per cent of its sales outside the USA. Although much smaller in the UK than Ford (with about 6000 employees), it is still one of our largest canned food producers.

Michelin (France) is one of the world's largest tyre producers, being the pioneer of radial tyres. It is also partly vertically integrated into rubber production and rubber products. It has factories in all the leading European and North American countries. It was established in 1893 and set up a sales subsidiary in the UK as early as 1905. Currently it is one of the largest tyre producers in this country, employing about 12000 workers.

Source: The International Directory of Company Histories, ed. Derdak, T., St James Press, Chicago and London, 1989, which is a remarkably detailed source of company histories of the world's leading companies.

Why are we interested?

Not surprisingly, these giant firms attract wide attention and controversy amongst economists, politicians and the media. At the political level there is concern about their accountability and loyalty to the countries in which they operate; and it is suggested that their size provides them with an irresistible power when bargaining with governments and/or labour unions. Some economists are also suspicious of the **monopoly power** that MNEs are reputed to possess and exploit to the detriment of potential competitors. These concerns surface most noticeably in the press when the larger multinationals embark on takeover quests with potential victims in other countries. In recent years UK firms have been frequently involved – either as the acquirers or as the acquired: Tables 2 and 3 cite some examples.

On the other hand the advocates of multinationals point to them as an important source of new employment, and argue that it is these firms which tend to be most innovative and efficient and to have the highest productivity levels.

The purpose of this book is to investigate some of these claims and counter-claims by examining the evidence. But we aim to provide more than just a 'fact-book'. As with most topics in economics, the facts only begin to make sense once one has a sound grasp of some of the theoretical issues involved. This is certainly true for multinationals, and what makes them so interesting to economists is that they are not easily analysed using the basic traditional models of economics.

When most of us are first confronted with the elementary theories of the firm and industry we are taught about **perfect competition,** in which there is a large number of small firms all producing the same homogeneous product. Apart from being small, these firms are also each supposed to operate a single plant (factory). This description is clearly quite inappropriate to MNEs. They usually operate many plants – indeed these plants are often located in many different countries. They will also usually produce a whole range of products – sometimes not even all in the same industry. So, far from being single-plant, single-product minnows, they are often multiplant, multiproduct, and multinational giants. And, far from being perfect competitors, they very often possess a considerable degree of monopoly or **oligopoly** power.

What this means is that we need a much wider and richer theoretical basis on which to found our examination of the facts; and this book is just as concerned with constructing that theoretical basis as with presenting the facts: both are equally important.

For this reason the next chapter takes us to the heart of the subject, by asking 'Why do multinational firms exist?' More precisely, the question

Table 2 Foreign firms' acquisitions in Britain, 1988–89

Target	Bidder	Nationality	Value (£million)
Rowntree	Nestlé	Swiss	2,622
Jaguar	Ford Motor	American	1,650
Inter-Continental Hotels	Seibu Saison	Japanese	1,350
Pearl Group	AMP	Australian	1,243
Morgan Grenfell	Deutsche Bank	West German	950
Metal Box Packaging	Carnaud	French	780
DRG	Pembridge Associates	American	640
RTZ Chemicals	Rhone-Poulenc	French	568
Rothmans International	Financiere Richemont	Swiss	543
RTZ Oil & Gas	Elf Aquitaine	French	308
Coates Brothers	Orkem	French	301
Peachey Property	Wereldhave	Dutch	281

Source: *Acquisitions Monthly*
NOTE: The table includes deals that are still pending.

Table 3 UK firms' acquisitions on the continent, 1988–89

Target	Nationality	Bidder	Value (£million)
Center Parks	Dutch	Scottish & Newcastle	518
Carat	French	WCRS	202
Banque de l'Union Européene	French	National Westminster	180
Elsevier	Dutch	Pearson	143
Newmont Mining (Oil & Gas)	Dutch	Clyde Petroleum	139
Flachglas	German	Pilkington	110
Sanitas	Spanish	Bupa	110
Lloyd Italico	Italian	Royal Insurance	98
Crest Hotels	German	Queens Moat Houses	96
Sema Metra	French	CAP Group	93

Source: *Acquisitions Monthly*

is why do firms choose to become multinational? The answers provided take us beyond the textbook world of perfect competition and free trade into the subject matter of modern industrial economics theory. Chapter 3 moves one stage on by examining the location decision: once a firm has chosen to become multinational, what determines *where* it chooses to locate, and *how* does it enter the foreign country? This involves questions of investment appraisal as well as locational economics. The following two chapters examine the effects of MNEs in the light of this theoretical background. Chapter 4 investigates macroeconomic issues such as the balance of payments, investment and employment, while Chapter 5 focuses more on the microeconomic questions of productivity, efficiency and wages. Chapter 6 considers the relationship between multinationals and host governments: in the light of the evidence and pros and cons of multinationals, what attitudes should governments adopt in their dealings with these firms? Finally, in Chapter 7 we embark on a little star-gazing by speculating upon some future developments which we believe to be likely in the coming years: there can be little doubt that the multinational firm is here to stay, the only question is just how dominant they are destined to become.

KEY WORDS

Multinational companies	Monopoly power
Multinational enterprises	Perfect competition
Home country	Oligopoly power
Host country	

Reading list

General information on multinational firms can be found in the pages of the business and quality newspapers, such as the *Independent*, *Financial Times*, *Economist*, *Times* etc. Company directories, such as the *Times 1000* (Times Books Ltd), *Kompass Directory* (Reed Information Services), *Who Owns Whom* (Dun and Bradstreet), may be used to establish the ownership and size of companies. The Annual Report and Accounts of individual companies should give details of their subsidiaries and the geographic spread of their operations.

Anderton, A.G., Work Card 6, 'Why Bowater is seeking the sun in Southern U.S.A.' in *Data Response Workpack in A-Level Economics*, UTP, 1985.

Davies, S. and Lund, M., 'MNEs: Some issues and facts', *Economic Review*, March 1989.

Foley, P., 'UK open for business', *Lloyds Bank Economic Bulletin*, June 1990.

Coursework topics

The objective of these questions is to acquaint students with the diversity of multinational firms and their relative importance in the United Kingdom economy. They require the use of data sources of various types, some of which are included in the reading list above. Local reference libraries may contain this material, and they may also keep other data, including files on individual local companies. Lists of companies are often produced and published by county and district councils. Work on the topics may be more efficient if it is preceded by a collective discussion that attempts to list foreign and UK multinational companies.

1. (a) Draw up a list of the larger firms within your local area and try to establish which of them are (i) subsidiaries of foreign multina tionals or (ii) UK firms with overseas activities.
   (b) Assess the relative importance of these multinational firms for the employment and economic activity within the local area.
   (c) To what extent does the multinational nature of these firms have implications for the health of the local economy?
2. Repeat Question 1 for a specific industry instead of a specific area.
3. Look at one week's issues of a quality newspaper that contains a substantial business section. List, document, and categorize all the items that relate to multinational firms. Write a short report on the extent of multinational operations and their impact on the economy, noting any areas that you feel are important but are not represented in the information that has been collected.

Chapter Two
Why do multinational firms exist?

'In 1976 it was possible to claim that "It is little exaggeration to say that at present there is no established theory of the multinational enterprise". The enormous output of theoretical work on the multinational enterprise since that date now makes this statement outdated.' P.J. Buckley, Chapter 2 of *The Growth of International Business*, ed. M. Casson, George Allen and Unwin, 1983

The answer to the chapter heading's question is central to any analysis of multinational enterprises (MNEs). Until we understand the motives firms have for setting up production capacity overseas – for 'going multinational' – it is difficult to ascertain the likely effects on both their host and home economies. Similarly, government policies aimed either at attracting new MNEs or regulating the operations of existing MNEs must be based on a recognition of those motives.

For this reason this chapter is the core one within the book: the various hypotheses that economists have evolved to explain why a firm may choose to go multinational can be seen to have been at play in explaining the examples introduced in the previous chapter, and they will reappear in subsequent chapters when we investigate the effects of MNEs.

Exporting versus overseas production
We start with an obvious statement, coupled with a more difficult question. The obvious statement is that any firm choosing to locate at least part of its operations overseas presumably wishes to sell its product(s) and/or service overseas. But the difficult question is why does it choose to *produce* overseas rather than merely *exporting* from its home base? After all, a Japanese car maker intent on selling to British consumers need not necessarily have factories in this country to persuade us to buy his product, rather than that of British-owned firms.

If we turn to traditional international trade theory we find no answer to the question. In the basic models of **comparative advantage** we find that countries specialize in producing those goods at which they are comparatively best, while relying on other countries to supply their needs in other goods. There is no point in firms locating overseas because all markets are assumed to be free of transport costs, supplied under conditions of constant returns to scale and perfect competition with homogeneous products. In short, traditional trade theory assumed **perfect markets**. It follows that if we are to understand why in fact some firms prefer to produce internationally in order to sell internationally we must look for some sort of **market imperfection**.

Tariff jumping and transport costs

Basic trade theory always assumes away the possibility of extra transport costs when supplying overseas markets, and ignores the possibility of **tariff protection**. Of course, both these market imperfections exist to varying degrees in most real world situations, and they provide an obvious reason why potential exporters may prefer to set up production in their overseas markets. This can be shown in the following simple model.

Assumptions

Consider a firm which produces a single good from a plant (factory) in its home country, and which initially sells the product at home and also exports to an overseas market.

The firm's costs involve a fixed element, F, and a marginal (or variable) cost, c, per unit of output produced. In turn, the fixed element represents two types of **fixed costs**:

- F1: initial outlays on research and development which are necessary to design the product in the first place, and
- F2: the outlays on land, buildings and plant necessary to set up the factory to produce the product.

The **marginal cost** represents material and labour costs. For simplicity, suppose that the magnitude of c is constant, whatever the scale of output. These assumptions imply that average costs will decline as scale increases (because the firm is able to spread the fixed cost over greater quantities), but the marginal cost curve is horizontal (because each *extra* unit produced costs the same amount, c). They also imply that the most efficient mode of operation is for the firm to concentrate its output in only one plant: multiplant operations would imply duplicating the fixed costs associated with factory construction. For this reason, one might expect the firm to operate only one plant (in its home country) from which it would supply all its customers, both home and overseas.

However, in order to export to the overseas market, the firm has to incur an additional constant marginal cost, t, which represents transport costs and any tariff imposed by the foreign government.

Turning to demand conditions, the home market has no interesting role to play in the analysis (since it will be unaffected by the firm's choice between exporting and 'going multinational', given the cost assumptions) and is therefore ignored hereafter. Figure 1 depicts only the outcome in the overseas market. The D˙D´ line represents the *demand curve for the firm's product* in the overseas market, and D´MR is the associated marginal revenue curve.

As for competition, we can either assume that the firm has a monopoly in the overseas market, or that there are indigenous domestic competitors. If it is to be the latter, we suppose that 'our' firm has a differentiated product such that it need not sell at the same price as competitors. In either case, the firm will face a downward sloping demand curve for its product, and if there is competition, this curve takes into account the behaviour of competitors.

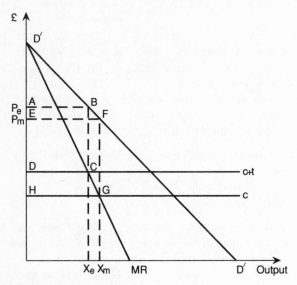

Figure 1 Exporting versus multinationality

Analysis

From the above assumptions, the firm's marginal costs of supplying this overseas market are c+t, shown by the horizontal line in Figure 1. Profit maximizing behaviour requires that the firm should supply the quantity at which marginal revenue equals marginal costs (i.e. X_e) and this corresponds to the price P_e. At this point, the firm's profits from the overseas market are given by the rectangle ABCD.

But now suppose the firm contemplates 'going multinational' by setting up a plant in the overseas country. From the above assumptions, this will affect costs in two ways. First transport costs and tariffs are avoided, thus reducing costs to c; second, it incurs an additional fixed cost, F2, which reflects the initial outlays on the new overseas factory (note, however, that there will be no need to replicate the original research and development, so F1 need not be incurred for a second time). Under these circumstances, because the marginal costs of supplying the overseas market are reduced to c, profit maximizing marginal revenue is lower, which requires an increase in output to X_m, and price falls to P_m. Variable profits are now the larger rectangle EFGH.

Conclusions

Although simple in the extreme, this model offers important insights into the circumstances under which the firm will go multinational and the sources of gains and losses to society if it does.

The firm will go multinational if the increase in variable profits exceeds the fixed cost of setting up the overseas plant. From the above, this condition is

$$EFGH - ABCD > F2$$

Now it is easily shown from elementary geometry that

$$EFGH - ABCD = DCGH$$

so the *condition for multinationality* is simply:

$$DCGH > F2$$

To interpret this condition, we need to identify what determines the magnitude of DCGH. From the diagram, we see that this is a trapezium, whose area depends on height (DH) and length (DC and HG). Since these reflect, in turn, the magnitudes of t, the tariff and transport costs, and X, output, it follows that firms are more likely to choose multinational production:

(a) where transport costs and tariffs are high,
(b) where a large output can be sold (i.e. where prospective markets are large).

Since the decision also depends on F2, the plant's fixed costs, a third factor making for multinational production is:

(c) where the fixed costs of setting up an additional plant are relatively low.

Note also that, where the firm does choose multinational production, it will produce a larger output and charge consumers a lower price than when it exports. In this sense, within the host country, consumers gain, and the balance of trade improves (owing to reduced imports), but the host government may lose through reduced tariff revenues, and host country competitors also presumably lose out on market share or profit margins, being now faced with a more efficient foreign competitor.

Source: *The Sunday Times*, 20 December 1987

Turning to the real world, this model explains, at least in part, the location of subsidiaries of Japanese and American companies in the UK, which thereby avoid the tariff barriers of the EEC and benefit from the increased effective size of the internal market with the removal of internal barriers to trade by 1992. Less obviously, it also points to certain types of industries which are more likely to be populated by multinationals. These are those which are 'large', involve a product which is costly to transport and/or is protected by tariffs, and for which fixed production (but not R&D) costs are relatively low. It also suggests that multinationals are a 'good thing'.

On the other hand, the model *is* very simplified and raises as many questions as it answers, as will become clear presently.

Overseas production to reduce production costs

In the above model we supposed that the firm's variable *production* costs were identical, at c, whether exporting from home or producing overseas (it was only in transport costs or tariffs that the two differed). In fact, there are good reasons for doubting this assumption.

To see why, note that production costs depend on (a) the technology, (b) the costs of the factors of production, and (c) the productivity or efficiency of those factors. Of these three it is really only the production technology itself which should be identical whether production is in the home or the host country (by and large, the multinational should be able to use the same technology in its plants wherever in the developed world they are located). But the other two determinants will usually differ to some extent between locations. Consider the efficiency of factors of production: while management and possibly capital equipment may be imported from the home country, and therefore are equally efficient in different locations, typically labour will differ in its efficiency between different countries (the most obvious reasons being differences in their education and training, but other national characteristics *may* mean that workers in some countries simply work harder or are more physically fit). Also, other intermediate inputs and components may differ in their quality between locations. But perhaps most important of all, factor prices are rarely equal in all countries. Indeed, international differences in factor prices have always been acknowledged in international trade theory as a major cause of trade, influencing comparative advantage.

In short, in the real world where factors of production are not perfectly mobile between nations, we should *expect* that the costs of production will invariably differ between locations. This then raises the real possibility that a firm may choose to locate production overseas to benefit from *lower production costs* due to cheaper and/or more efficient factors of production. If this is so, then the marginal cost curve for overseas production will be lower, and the gains from multinationality larger, than originally shown in our figure. This certainly accords with a popular perception that many UK multinationals switch their output overseas to benefit from cheaper labour costs (examples include TVs, shoes and textiles produced in the third world but sold in this country under UK brand names). But this possibility raises another question to be answered. If multinational firms can benefit in the form of cheaper factor costs from locating in an overseas country, then domestic firms from that country must also surely benefit in the same way. If so, what need is there for multinational firms to exploit these lower costs in the host country? To answer this, we must now turn to the dominant theoretical explanation of multinationals.

The specific advantage

It is now widely accepted amongst economists that MNEs are firms possessing some **specific advantage** relative to other producers, either in their home or host country.

The precise nature of this advantage will differ between cases, and we shall provide some examples presently. The logic of the argument is simple, however, and is based on the recognition that any firm operating outside its home environment will probably start with an inbuilt handicap *vis-à-vis* its domestic competitors. It may be less familiar with consumer tastes, social and cultural conditions in the host country, and/ or have less knowledge of the factor markets in which it will buy, or the product markets in which it will sell. It stands to reason, then, that only those foreign firms which also have some peculiar advantage, to counteract these handicaps, will contemplate setting up production overseas.

Perhaps the most obvious type of advantage is the technological. The multinational firm may produce an inherently superior (probably patented) product, or use production processes which are superior to those of its domestic competitors. Richard Caves, a leading contemporary advocate of this explanation, argues that **product differentiation** is the main source of these technological advantages – and, of course, they are clearly inconceivable in the abstract textbook world of perfect competition in which all firms produce the same homogeneous product using the same process of production. This differentiation may be due to physical differences (i.e. different technical characteristics) of the product; for example, better designed motor cars, or tractors, machine tools which are technically superior to the products of domestic firms. Usually, this will occur in industries where the technical capabilities of the product or design are important, and this may be the result of innovation from research and development expenditures. In other cases, however, the advantage may be more intangible, and to do with the **brand image**: this might be true for soft drinks, cigarettes, cosmetics, breakfast cereals etc. Often the multinational will sell using a widely recognized brand name (or names), which usually will have been created and consolidated by persistent, heavy advertising.

Another important type of specific advantage is greater **entrepreneurial and managerial skills**. Here, the firm expands overseas in order to exploit some unusual organizational or entrepreneurial skills of its management. Essentially, this is what many people have in mind when assessing the particular advantages of Japanese firms setting up production in the UK and introducing better work practices than indigenous firms. In earlier decades this was often argued as the major advantage of US multinationals in Europe.

It should be stressed, however, that a specific advantage alone is not sufficient to explain multinational production. In addition three other conditions are necessary:

(a) the asset must be transferable more or less intact and relatively cheaply from one country to another,
(b) it must be difficult for domestic firms to emulate, and
(c) overseas production must be more profitable than other modes of selling overseas, namely exporting directly or licensing to a domestic producer.

The first two conditions are fairly obvious. For example, if Japanese firms are unable, for some reason, to exploit their better organizational and work practice skills in the British environment, they would lose their advantage over indigenous British producers, and the point of overseas production would be lost. Similarly, there would be little point in a French tyre producer setting up production in the UK if British manufacturers were able to copy exactly the specification of their tyres and also completely counteract the brand image of the French MNE. These specific examples could refer respectively to Nissan and Michelin – both of whom produce in the UK precisely because they are able to transfer their specific advantages without British firms being able to emulate them perfectly.

The third condition deserves a fuller discussion. We have already seen in the figure how overseas production will be preferred to exporting where transport costs and tariffs are large relative to the fixed cost of setting up production overseas. But if we now introduce the notion that the firm concerned possesses a specific advantage, the analysis can be deepened. In particular, does the firm need to set up overseas to exploit its advantage, or will exporting do as well? There is no general answer to this question: it will depend on the specific case being considered. For example, stylish Italian suits may be sold in the British marketplace without the manufacturers having to produce them in Britain. This is an example where the specific advantage (superior styling) does not require local production to be exploited. The same is true of high-technology machine tools produced in Germany and sold by exporting (through agents) in the UK and throughout Europe. On the other hand, American car producers have long since preferred to penetrate overseas markets by producing internationally rather than by exporting. Undoubtedly, part of the reason for this was the heavy transport costs, but also important was the recognition that American and European consumers had different tastes. In order to be responsive to those tastes it was felt necessary to have local production units producing cars with styling different from those sold to American consumers; and production close to the overseas marketplace was seen as the best way of keeping in touch with, and helping to influence, those local tastes. Similarly, local production was seen as beneficial to creating and monitoring local sales outlets, after-sales service etc.

In fact there is a third option when selling overseas: allowing a local producer to produce and sell your product under licence. This mode has been used by, for example, Coca Cola, and is currently the practice with various European lagers produced under licence by UK brewers. The advantage here is that one has a production base close to the marketplace without necessarily incurring all the fixed costs of setting up from scratch. On the other hand, where the specific advantage arises from informational factors, such as secret know-how and/or advanced techniques, the danger with licensing is that the licensee must be provided with that information, in which case the advantage is no longer specific, and the risk is that the licensee may later set up on his own and imitate the product.

The product cycle

The specific advantage theme is further developed in the theory of the **product cycle**. This was designed specifically with innovation and research and development in mind. The theory was stimulated by the observation that most new products or processes are first developed and introduced by firms in the rich developed countries. But as the processes/products proceed through various stages in their life cycle, there sometimes comes a time when it is most efficient for the innovating firms to switch production overseas, i.e. to go multinational.

The hypothesis that firms in the richer developed countries have the strongest incentives and capabilities to make major new labour-saving technologies is certainly borne out by the facts. The theoretical explanation is that innovations are typically labour-saving and initially expensive, and therefore most attractive to consumers in the developed world with higher incomes, and where labour is most costly. (Here we should interpret labour as either labour in the home or at the workplace. In the home, consumer durables such as washing machines are devices which release housewives or househusbands from housework and allow them to take up outside paid employment; for them it is the **opportunity cost** of housework which is high. In the industrial context, a new process of production for the firm, such as industrial robots, permits it to reduce the workforce by effectively substituting capital for labour.)

Given that a firm (or firms) in a developed nation has made such an innovation (i.e. established a specific advantage), the life cycle of the new product/process is described by four stages.

Stage 1 is the initial stage of introduction in which the innovating firm chooses to produce in its home country. At this stage, sales are unlikely to be substantial and the firm's main concern is to concentrate on those consumers who are relatively wealthy and who are more concerned with the technical specification and capability of the product rather than its price. As such, the main concern is to be in close proximity to those 'adventurous' consumers in order to be able to monitor their reactions, and change the specification of the innovation in the light of consumers' experiences with it. Because price is less important than quality improvements the innovator is less concerned with his costs and so, although producing at home may not be necessarily the most cost-efficient option (compared with a lower-labour-cost overseas location), this is less important than the technical advantages in a home location.

Stage 2 sees the innovator learning about his innovation: early teething troubles are ironed out, and the new product becomes more mature. This has a number of implications. First, as the market builds up, the firm is able to introduce more standardized production techniques; second, it may begin to sell in export markets; and third, other firms may begin to imitate. For each of these reasons the selling price of the product becomes more important, as does the need to look for cost reductions.

Stage 3 sees the possibility that the firm might best be advised to locate some of its production overseas. Again, this may be for a number of reasons. Scale economies from producing at home may have been exhausted, so an overseas plant may become at least equally efficient as the original home one(s). Moreover, there may be positive reasons for locating additional capacity in the overseas market: perhaps to evade tariffs that overseas governments begin to impose on the product as it gains ground, and/or because there may be selling advantages in having the plant close to overseas consumers.

Stage 4 occurs when overseas operations may be expanded at the expense of home operations. For example, a factory in overseas country A may be used to supply consumers not only in A, but also in overseas country B. Indeed in some cases, the overseas factory may be used to supply consumers in the home country of the firm. The main reason for this will be lower labour costs (remembering that the home country of the multinational will usually be a high-income/high-labour-cost country). At this stage in the life of the product, with all the major technological features established, it may be the cost of standard factors of production, rather than the availability of highly skilled workers so necessary in the early stages, which are of most importance.

A more critical view

So far the overriding theme of these various hypotheses is that the firm's decision to opt for international production is determined by considerations of efficiency, and this tends to imply that multinationals are a 'good thing' in helping to secure the best possible utilization of scarce resources. There is, however, another side to the question, when firms choose the multinational option for less acceptable reasons than those so far discussed. We shall mention three such cases.

Some economists, especially those of Marxist persuasions, suggest that a major reason for multinational operations is the firm's desire to 'control the labour process'. The details of this argument would require more space than is available here, but at its heart is a simple point. When dealing with its workforce, a firm may find it useful to fragment that workforce into smaller groups, especially if those groups are geographically dispersed.

In fact, the argument can be explained using the terms and tools of conventional neo-classical economics. Consider the example of negotiations between an employer and a trade union over rates of pay or rewards for effort and productivity. In a world of perfectly competitive labour markets, the terms of the labour bargain are dictated largely by market forces, and no one firm, or group of workers, is sufficiently large to influence them. But many real world labour markets are far from perfect: on the one hand, the firm (employer) accounts for a large proportion of demand in the given industry and/or geographical locality, and on the other hand, the supply of labour is controlled to a greater or lesser extent by a monopoly union. This constitutes the classic conditions for what economists refer to as **bilateral monopoly**, i.e. a monopoly buyer (monopsonist) dealing with a monopoly supplier. In these circumstances the price (which is here the wage rate since we are considering the market for labour) must be determined by a bilateral bargain between the two parties, and just how that bargain is settled will depend on the relative strengths of the two parties.

Now if the employer is able to fragment its workers across a number of different plants, each of which it negotiates with separately, this reduces the bargaining strength of each labour group. This is not only because the threats of each group (such as strikes or other forms of labour action) are less powerful if only confined to one factory, but also because the employer may be able to play one group off against another. This 'divide and rule' strategy may be seen most obviously in those cases where a firm, faced with a militant group of workers in one factory, threatens to switch production to its factories elsewhere. Notice that this strategy requires more than just splitting operations between a number of plants – they must also be spread across different countries, i.e. the firm must be multinational. This is because it will only succeed if the workers in different factories are unable to collude amongst themselves and deal in unison with the employer. This is precisely what happens within the UK: it is the norm in most British companies for wage negotiations to be conducted more or less at the national level, with unions negotiating on behalf of workers in all plants. It is far less usual, indeed very rare, at the international level: nearly all multinational firms bargain with different unions in each of the countries in which they operate.

A second cynical motive sometimes ascribed to MNEs is *international production to secure preferential treatment from host governments*. The argument is similar to that above, but this time with the multinational firm playing one government off against another. It rests on the fairly frequent tendency of governments to offer major overseas firms various inducements to locate new factories in their country. These inducements may include (i) favourable interest rates and credit conditions, (ii) tax differentials and incentives, and (iii) depreciation allowances, and they tend to be most common in either developing countries anxious to promote development, or in developed countries keen to attract new industry to declining regions. It is argued that a multinational firm has more scope for driving a hard bargain with host countries than do domestic firms, precisely because they always have the option of taking their factories elsewhere. Nor need this type of strategy be confined to a multinational contemplating first-time entry – it may also be used when deciding where to locate expansions of existing operations. In principle this strategy could be employed by any firm, and not just those already multinational. In practice, however, the fact that a firm is already multinational makes a threat to locate in another country more credible than where the firm is at present confined to a single country, and therefore lacking the experience of overseas operations.

Market power motives

As will be seen in Chapter 5, invariably multinational firms tend to operate in highly concentrated industries, i.e. where there are relatively few competitors, corresponding to **oligopoly**. In these circumstances it is natural to ask whether a firm's decision to operate multinationally is motivated by a desire to increase its **market power**. If so, multinationality may lead to higher prices to the detriment of consumers. This suspicion is often voiced in popular discussions, and it has also attracted increasing attention in modern oligopoly theory. Here we shall make a few suggestive observations. The first derives from the earlier diagram (Figure 1) describing the export versus overseas production decision; we saw that a firm will sell more in an overseas market if producing locally than if exporting, because of the lower marginal costs in the absence of tariffs and transport costs in the former. In turn, this may make it more difficult for domestic firms to compete with a multinational than with imports, eventually resulting in their leaving the industry. In the short run this will have no detrimental effects as far as consumers are concerned – after all, if domestic firms do exit this is precisely the result of the greater efficiency of the multinational. However, in the longer run, with domestic competition removed, the multinational may be able to move to a monopoly position and raise price.

We should note, however, that this scenario does require that the multinational firm is able to erect **entry barriers** to prevent new domestic (or indeed foreign) entry when it subsequently raises price. While this may not always be possible, the very fact that multinationals often operate in industries subject to product differentiation, which requires substantial outlays on research and development and/or advertising, is important. Very often these outlays are by their nature a **sunk cost**

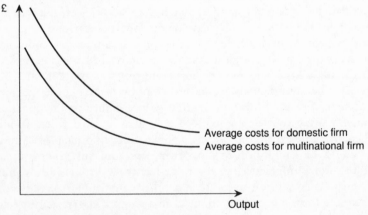

Figure 2 The cost advantage of multinationals

which means that potential competitors will be loathe to enter unless they are sure of being able to recoup those costs. In this respect entry into an overseas country by a multinational is not identical to the entry of a new domestic firm. While in both cases the firm must incur the same outlays on physical plant (F2 in the earlier example), it is only the domestic firm which must incur the outlays on R&D and product differentiation – the multinational already having incurred these in its home operations (see Figure 2). This is not so much an *unfair* advantage of multinationals but more of an explanation of why multinationals may be able to enter and survive where domestic firms cannot. If this argument is accepted then the implication is that the multinational, once entered, may have the potential to exploit a market to the detriment of consumers.

This issue is particularly important if we consider the means by which a multinational firm sets up production overseas: is it by establishing an entirely new factory (greenfield entry) or by acquiring (i.e. taking over) an existing domestic firm? The implications for competition may be different. In the greenfield case, entry means either the addition of a new seller into the market, or the replacement of imports by lower-cost local production. Either way this must surely increase competition (at least in the short run). But where the entry is by acquisition of an existing local rival, competition may be reduced. Loosely speaking this distinction can be applied to two major entries of multinationals into the UK in recent years: Nissan's greenfield entry into the UK car industry, as opposed to Nestlé's expansion into confectionery by the acquisition of Rowntree Mackintosh.

Different types of overseas production
Most of the above theories are most directly relevant to **horizontal** multinational production, that is, a firm producing essentially the same products in different countries: Ford being a classic example. They are also generally applicable to **conglomerate** multinationals, i.e. firms producing different goods in different countries. A third category which deserves special attention, however, is **vertical** multinationals. These are firms which produce raw materials or intermediate inputs in one country, which are then used in the production of a final product in another country. While quantitatively less important than the other types of multinationals, such firms are certainly significant in the British context. Historically, a number of British firms felt it necessary to control their own supplies of metals, minerals, wool, cotton etc. from overseas continents. Once more, the question arises: why did they choose to produce overseas rather than merely importing from foreign companies? In fact

part of the answer lies with the above hypotheses – market power considerations, the desire to exploit their own perceived specific advantages (i.e. better management technique). But in addition, removal of uncertainty about supplies was also a factor.

KEY WORDS

Comparative advantage	Product cycle
Perfect markets	Opportunity cost
Market imperfections	Bilateral monopoly
Tariff protection	Oligopoly
Fixed costs	Market power
Marginal cost	Entry barriers
Specific advantage	Sunk cost
Product differentiation	Horizontal
Brand image	Conglomerate
Entrepreneurial and managerial skills	Vertical

Reading list
Casson, M. (ed.), *The Growth of International Business*, George Allen & Unwin, 1983.

Coursework topic
Try to find a company history and use it to assess the underlying rationale for the overseas expansion of the company concerned.

Essay topics
1. To what extent are economies of scale and the introduction of new technology the motivating force for multinational expansion?
2. 'Nothing has undermined the hypothesis that companies expand abroad simply to maximize profits'. Discuss.
3. How would you explain the considerable increase in the multinational operations of companies in the service industries over the last twenty years?
4. Explain what the economist means by 'a firm' and why organizations as diverse as ICI and a corner shop can be said to possess the same essential characteristics from the economic viewpoint. (Joint Matriculation Board, June 1987)
5. How does oligopoly differ from monopoly? (University of Oxford Delegacy of Local Examinations, June 1987)

Data Response Question 1
Japanese Investment Overseas
The discussion in the text above has concentrated on the reasons for individual firms expanding overseas. In modern times the pre-conditions for overseas expansion can apply to whole industries, or to whole countries. Read the passage below, taken from an article in the *Financial Times* of 7 December 1988, and then answer the following questions.

1. Explain the terms 'international currency alignments', 'labour-intensive', 'trade barriers', 'dumping', 'capacity', 'product strategies', and 'up-market'.
2. What are the general conditions that have led to the recent overseas expansion of Japanese industry?
3. What sort of industries would you expect to have been particularly affected by this expansion?
4. What difficulties have the Japanese companies found in their host countries?

JAPANESE INDUSTRY
Investment in overseas production rises rapidly

'The battleground between Japanese companies has now shifted to manufacturing overseas. Most of them know that continuing to rely on exports just won't work in future', says Mr. Alan Bell, vice-president of research at the Tokyo office of Salomon Brothers, the US Investment Bank.

The main initial stimulus to the recent surge of foreign manufacturing investment was the sharp rise in the yen following the Plaza Agreement on international currency realignments in the autumn of 1985.

That led many Japanese companies to shift production of basic products and simpler components to low-cost south east Asian locations. Because such plants are often heavily labour-intensive, the companies have continued to switch production from country to country in response to movements in relative exchange rates.

In the industrialized world, trade barriers, or the threat of them, have provided a powerful additional impetus. Many Japanese companies have set up European assembly plants after dumping duties were imposed on their exports, while the rush into US car manufacturing was triggered largely by the 1981 voluntary export restraints demanded by the Reagan Administration.

This transfer of capacity has often involved formidable management challenges. As well as having to find alternative employment for workers at home, Japanese companies have often complained bitterly about the difficulty of achieving overseas high levels of quality and cost.

Some of these teething troubles are undoubtedly due to Japanese companies' failure to adapt to local conditions. They have often built overseas plants which

25

were exact replicas of those at home without first considering whether suitable local supplies were available to make them work.

Some Japanese copier companies found their US plants were unable to use American grades of aluminium, so they ended up importing the metal from Japan at huge extra cost. Subsequent plants have been re-designed to accept local sources of aluminium.

Despite such hurdles, much of Japanese industry believes it has no choice but to persist with overseas expansion if it is to remain competitive. Alps, for instance, says that by producing in Europe it can meet in two months orders which would take four months to fill if supplied from Japan.

An increasingly important motive is a continuing shift in Japanese companies' product strategies. As they move up-market into more complicated and sophisticated products, they are finding that their customers' requirements oblige them to invest in a more extensive local presence.

Data Response Question 2
The National Diamond

This chapter has discussed ideas on why multinational firms exist. The following review by Peter Williamson of Professor Porter's book *The Competitive Advantage of Nations*, published in the *Times* of 25 July 1990, seems to be concerned with a different topic. Or is it? Read the passage and then answer the following questions.

1. To what extent are the factors accounting for the competitive advantage of nations discussed in the passage the same as those discussed in this chapter as explanations for the emergence of a multinational firm? What are the implications of your findings?
2. Can you find any industries for which the 'cluster' argument seems not to apply?
3. Examine the logic of the last paragraph of the passage.

Tough time at home helps you to shine abroad

The Competitive Advantage of Nations (Macmillan, £25) pulls off the seemingly impossible. It adds a fresh dimension to the international competitiveness debate, which has been going on since Adam Smith and David Ricardo.

Mr. Porter begins by pointing out that we have been asking the wrong question. The issue is not why one nation cannot compete with another but rather, why there are concentrations of firms in a particular business.

Why is tiny Switzerland the home base for international leaders in pharmaceuticals and chocolate? Why is Britain the home of the dominant companies in international auctioneering and biscuits? Put that way, what might have looked like the topic of a boring chancellor's speech is transformed into global competitive strategy after all.

Question in hand, Mr. Porter goes off in search of clusters of corporate successes in Denmark, West Germany, Italy, Japan, Korea, Singapore, Sweden, Switzerland, Britain and America. Successful exporters and foreign investors are usually found together in local tribes instead of scattered around the globe. Understanding their social habits involves case studies of more than a hundred industries, from food additives in Denmark to pianos in Korea and syringes in the US.

Much of the value of the conclusions come from the fact that they are often counter-intuitive. We all know the leaders in an industry are found where the raw materials, labour or other inputs required are cheap and abundant. The trouble is, we find the chocolate leaders in Switzerland, not the obvious place to take advantage of a supply of cocoa beans.

It turns out that in the age of advanced transport and the global company, endowments of inputs rank way down the list of contributors to national advantage.

Another piece of oft-quoted wisdom is that scale economies, arising from a few large players sharing the national market, will promote an internationally competitive industry.

Mr. Porter finds the opposite. Intense competition in the home market drives businesses to faster technological improvement, higher quality and better marketing. Once overseas, they win hands down, finding the foreign competitive bouts are not as tough as their training matches at home.

How many executives pray for the godsend of really difficult customers, always asking for something different and more complicated?

Yet, Mr. Porter finds the most successful international players are those with the most sophisticated and demanding home buyers. Under continuous pressure for higher quality, greater variety and more new products, that is just what they deliver. These forces – input conditions, competitive rivalry and customer sophistication, with the quality of ancillary industries – are boiled down into what Mr. Porter christens the 'National Diamond'.

In its virtuous guise, the diamond forms a dynamic spiral of productivity improvement, which contributes to world success for corporation and country. Missing one of its key molecules, however, the diamond is prone to turn to dust.

More and more companies are looking to subsidiaries in Japan or West Germany because to be successful in a global market, one needs to ensure contact with the most demanding customers, the best suppliers worldwide and the toughest rivals.

Data Response Question 3
The reasons for overseas expansion
The discussion in the text has provided considerable detail on the motives for firm expansion abroad. In the passage that follows, Patrick Foley, Deputy Chief Economic Adviser of Lloyds Bank, writing in the Lloyds Bank *Economic Bulletin*, June 1990, provides a more concentrated version of the argument. Read the passage, and then answer the following questions.

1. Explain the terms 'higher income stream', 'cost of capital', 'portfolio investment', 'market breakdown', and 'non-tariff trade barriers'.
2. Why is it possible that foreign firms might expect a higher income stream from a project than domestic firms would expect?
3. To what extent can the reasons for overseas production discussed in the text of this chapter be classified into Mr. Foley's categories of monopolistic power and market breakdown? Are there any arguments in the text that cannot be pigeon-holed in this way?

The Economics of Inward Investment

Why would a firm want to invest in production overseas, and why is domestic industry not prepared to make the same investment? First, the foreign firm may expect a higher income stream from the project. Second, for the same income stream, it may have a lower cost of capital. Theory suggests that the first reason is more likely to be important than the second. After all, if cost of capital was the dominant reason, why should foreign firms not simply indulge in portfolio investment(*) in the country concerned, and save themselves the extra costs and uncertainties that come with direct investment?

Hence, the dominant direct investment incentive for overseas firms is that they believe they can make superior profits to domestic industry. Obviously, in a world of perfect competition, this would not be possible, and this implies that it is monopolistic power and other forms of market breakdown that create the incentive. In this area, the most important forms of monopoly power probably result either from economies of scale or from superior production techniques. The most important forms of market breakdown are probably non-tariff trade barriers or natural barriers to trade such as exist for some service sectors. To take the example of the 1992 initiative, this is likely to create the incentive for direct investment by European industry to take advantage of economies of scale, and by non-European industry to bypass external barriers to trade in the single market.

* Explanatory note: Portfolio investment in this context would refer to the foreign firm purchasing a selection of stocks and shares in a variety of domestic firms, without necessarily taking them over.

Chapter Three
The location decision

*'The choice of a new location for an industrial investment is not a task to
be undertaken lightly by the management of any company, public or
private.'* P.M. Townroe

The nature of the decision
The previous chapter concentrated on the underlying motives for firms
'going multinational'. In practice, once the first decision to expand
abroad has been taken a host of further questions arise. Should the firm
set up an entirely new operation – a **'greenfield'** site – or should it merge
with or take over an existing company in another country? Which is the
most appropriate continent or country to move into? Where is the best
location in a particular country? How does this decision dovetail with
other international ventures that have already taken place, or are in
prospect? These are the kinds of questions considered in this chapter.

Of course some of these decisions may already have been circumscribed by the force that is driving the firm into expansion. It may have
discovered a new bauxite deposit, acquired a technological advantage in a
sophisticated industrial product, embarked on a global strategy for the
production and sale of a consumer product, or decided to move production to an area of cheap labour. In each case the underlying logic of the
expansion will constrain the range of alternatives open to the firm.
Nevertheless, a large number of possibilities may remain and in some
way it will have to choose between them.

If we accept the central tenet of the economic theory of the firm, that
its objective is the maximization of profits, then in its expansion a multinational firm spends money now in the expectation that this will generate
increased profits in the future. It may invest a considerable amount of
capital in setting up a manufacturing branch three thousand miles away,
or will make an expensive contested takeover bid for 'Ozone
Replenishment Plc' in Utopia. It takes such actions to increase its size
and raise its profits. 'Pay now, profit later' should be its motto. This
means that the firm's decision to expand abroad is essentially an investment. It is just the same process as spending money on a new piece of
machinery, a new building, or the development of a new product. The
only difference is that this project is much larger, more expensive, and

more complicated. Nevertheless the same rules should be followed. The firm should consider a number of possible actions and select the best, or most profitable, option in a logical manner. In other words, it should use the standard techniques of investment appraisal.

Investment appraisal

Of the many techniques of investment appraisal available economists tend to advocate methods based on the process of discounting. **Discounting** is based on the principle of **compound interest**, which can be explained as follows. If you have £20 million to spare you can deposit that money in a financial institution and it will earn interest. Suppose that the interest rate is 12 per cent a year. At the end of the first year your capital sum will still be available, but the bank will also pay you £2.4 million interest. The amount left on deposit is now £22.4 million, or £20(1+0.12) million. If you leave this larger sum on deposit for a second year, it will acquire another 12 per cent interest and thus increase to £25.088 million. This is equivalent to £(22.4+2.688) million, or £20(1+0.12)(1+0.12) million, or £20(1+0.12)^2 million. The general formula states that if you deposit an amount A in an account that pays interest at an annual rate of r per cent, then, at the end of t years, the value of your deposit will have increased to $A(1 + r)^t$, presuming that you leave the money in all the time.

As a result of this process it can be seen that, essentially, the two sums of money, £20 million now, and £25.088 million available at the end of two years, are the same, as long as the annual rate of interest is 12 per cent. The £20 million available now could always be converted to the larger sum available in the future. On the other hand, the guarantee of £25.088 million available in two years time is equivalent to having £20 million now. As £25.088 million equals £20(1 +0.12)^2 million the appropriate method of converting it to the £20 million it is worth today, its 'present value', is to divide it by $(1 + 0.12)^2$. This is the process known as 'discounting a future sum back to its present value'. In general, a future sum A_t available in t years time may be discounted back to its present value A_0 by dividing it by $(1 + r)^t$. That is, $A_0 = A_t/(1 + r)^t$, where A_0 is the present value of A_t and r is the **discount rate**.

This procedure provides the basis for some quite refined methods of investment appraisal. The core of the argument is that the firm should estimate the initial cost involved, say A_0, as well as the stream of future annual profits expected from the investment, A_1, A_2, etc. for a fixed lifespan of n years. Each of these future profit streams should be discounted by the appropriate discount rate $(1 + r)^t$, and they should then be summed. If the sum of the discounted flow of future profits exceeds the initial expenditure, the project is worth undertaking. That is, the criterion is whether or not the sum of $A_1/(1 + r)$ plus $A_2/(1 + r)^2$ plus $A_3/(1 + r)^3$ etc. exceeds A_0.

The difficulties involved

The description above belies the considerable complexities in estimation and calculation often needed to carry out such methods in practice. To estimate future profits one needs projections of future sales revenue and costs, and inevitably these estimates will be very uncertain. The firm may view the whole project as very risky and wish to build in some risk factor. The selection of the appropriate discount rate is also unclear, depending upon the rate of interest and the cost of capital to the firm. In addition, management may determine that they should at least break even within a short time horizon, such as three to five years, regardless of the life of the project. Moreover, these complexities apply to the calculation for each single project but the multinational firm might be considering say, three sites in each of five countries. In theory it should make detailed estimates for each of the fifteen possibilities, and only after that work has been completed should a decision be made.

Actual practice

It is doubtful that prospective multinational firms go to quite the lengths implied by such methods of investment appraisal, although they may spend considerable time and money in researching the potential of alternative sites and companies. They will probably start with a preliminary sifting of possible projects, countries and locations on a subjective or intuitive basis, with detailed appraisal techniques only being used at a later stage, after the awkward decisions have been made. However, note that this initial subjective evaluation may all too easily degenerate into the effects of personal whims. Having made a decision to locate within the European Community an American business may automatically plump for England – after all they speak a form of American there – rather than West Germany, which is where all the customers and the growth is.

Greenfield site or takeover?

An initial decision that firms face is whether to expand by setting up some entirely new venture from scratch, the greenfield site option, or whether to expand by taking over, or merging with, an existing local venture. For some types of industries and projects these decisions will be foregone conclusions. In the case of the classical colonial company, solely concerned with the exploitation of a local indigenous resource such as a tin deposit (also see the Case Studies in Chapter 1), the decision was sometimes simplified by the total absence of local producers. Having found the tin deposit the problem is how best to exploit it, and that means starting from scratch. Again, for manufacturing multinationals considering operations in less developed countries a greenfield site may also be the only possibility. There will not be the home producers ripe for **takeover** and a completely new operation is the only answer.

A similar type of foregone conclusion, but this time leading towards a **merger** or takeover, arises from the modern trend to the expansion of service companies, particularly in those cases that depend upon a network of outlets, such as retail stores, vehicle distribution or insurance. In these cases the logistical problems of setting up a network of operations throughout a new area will usually make it preferable to take over an existing firm and its network. Setting up a chain of fifty shops in a foreign country is rarely a feasible task, and certainly not in the short term.

Between these extremes there arise many cases, particularly for manufacturing firms operating in developed countries, where there are real choices to be made. A factor that will usually be of particular importance in that choice is the nature of the market for the product. Suppose that there are two possibilities: production in and for the market of a specific country, such as the United Kingdom; or production in one country but with the expectation of exporting within a region, such as the European Community. The latter strategy may apply particularly to existing large multinational corporations that see the world as their market and plan their expansion from a global viewpoint.

In the first case the firm is probably trying to enter an oligopolistic market in which competition is already intense. Of course, the existence of its multinational dimension suggests that it may have specific advantages as described in Chapter 2; of product, technology or marketing expertise. Nevertheless, it will be faced by entry barriers such as the need to produce at the 'minimum economic size' determined by economies of scale (i.e. at or beyond point M on Figure 3). If entry is made with an output of less than M the costs of production will stop the entrant being competitive. To enter and be competitive the firm must acquire economies of scale by producing an output greater than M, the minimum economic size.

On the other hand, the introduction of an additional firm of large size into a national market could start a price war leading to the bankruptcy of one or more firms in the market, not excluding the possibility that this could be the multinational itself. In these circumstances, entry by buying an existing firm in the market may be much safer than setting up a new greenfield operation.

Entry for production and sale on a more global basis may bias the company towards a greenfield site operation. One factor in this decision may be the attitudes of, and incentives provided by, governments. They may accept such an operation with enthusiasm; not only will there be the multiplier effects of setting up the plant but there will also be additional employment in the longer term. As well as increasing competition in the domestic industry, and thus benefiting local consumers, it will also generate additional exports and improve the balance of payments. It is far better that such a plant should be in your country than sited elsewhere. It was probably such sentiments that led the United Kingdom government to welcome the establishment of the Nissan and Toyota car manufacturing plants (see pages 34 and 35).

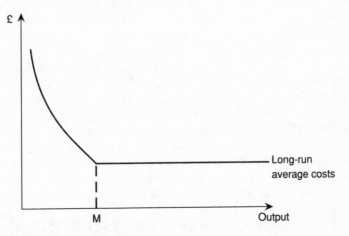

Figure 3 Minimum economic size

The nature of the appraisal

Ostensibly the takeover decision is the easier to assess. The number of potential candidate companies for acquisition may be established quite easily and the investment decision is then simply a question of deciding the worth of each business to you, the price you would be willing to pay for it, and the price that the company will be willing to be sold for. These are matters of business finance, accounting, and market research, and they avoid some of the nasty problems of the greenfield option, such as finding the sites, establishing the network of suppliers and the channels of delivery, finding the workforce, and installing all the machinery etc. On the other hand they introduce other problems, such as mounting a takeover battle, possible government interference on either political or monopoly grounds, and eventually adapting your victim and its workforce to your own products and practices. Experience shows that a high proportion of takeovers fail to fulfil the profit expectations of the initiating company. Takeover raiders almost always underestimate the problems involved in turning round or adapting an established company, or they overestimate their own competence in doing so. Merger is rarely the easy option it seems.

On the other hand starting from a greenfield site is also far from easy. In this case there is the need to establish possible site options, their costs, advantages and disadvantages. Each possible site may be viewed as a node that is linked to a very wide range of customers, employees, suppliers etc. Not only is there the need to investigate the production costs at the node, with such costs as finding and training the new workforce, installing the machinery and equipment etc., but there are also all the **transaction costs** involved in negotiations with trade unions, establishing the contracts necessary to tie up sub-contractors and suppliers of components, establishing the network of customers etc. For a multinational company important **linkages** may involve its other subsidiary firms, research and development sites abroad, and the headquarters thousands of miles away. Such international links will tend to push the location towards an international airport, and away from a low-cost labour location. Finally, when setting up in a strange location a firm is faced with a spectrum of legal and socio-economic problems, such as tax and social security payments, health and safety at work legislation, environmental problems etc. Faced with these difficulties firms may well resort to the takeover option, since these problems will have already been resolved by the company which is to be acquired.

Factories in regions give Japanese a high profile

Most Japanese investment in Britain has been in the financial or property sectors, and has been absorbed into the City or South-east with hardly a mention in the Press. Japanese sales operations are strung out along the Thames Valley – near airports and motorways – and again attract little comment.

Factories are another matter, however. They are high profile: new factories have been rare enough in the past decade, and the Japanese have built a fair share of those that have appeared. Furthermore, they have moved into areas that everyone else has been abandoning: most stories

about Japanese investment are stories about the North-east or South Wales.

The statistics show that there is an element of myth even here. Of the 129 actual or proposed Japanese factories listed in the latest edition of *Japanese Business and Investment* (produced by The Economic Develop-ment Briefing), only 17 are in South Wales and 19 are in the North-east.

When Toyota announced a year ago that it was setting up in Derbyshire, much was made of the fact that the Japanese had shied away from the heavily unionized Midlands in the past. In fact, 19 companies are based in the West Midlands – the same as in the North-east. More surprising still, 18 factories are in south central or south-eastern England.

Nevertheless, there is evidence that Japanese companies tend to cluster together. Of the 19 West Midlands-based companies, 10 are in Telford, and there are other concentrations in Wrexham, mid-Glamorgan and County Durham/-Sunderland. Toyota is building such a large factory that it deliberately chose to be away from other Japanese motor manufacturers – it did not want to recruit in the same pool – but there is little doubt that other Japanese companies will now start looking in the Derby area

It is debatable how far this clustering is a normal attribute of inward investment, and how far it is specifically a Japanese phenomenon. Much of the investment has clearly been influenced by regional grants. Telford is a new town with a battery of incentives; smaller Japanese concentra-tions are to be found in Milton Keynes and the Scottish new towns, while the North-east and South Wales have development status.

The attraction of high unemployment areas with a huge pool of workers is clear to major employers like Nissan, which set up in Sunderland. The level of unionization is barely relevant, however: all big companies prefer to recruit young workers who can be instilled with their own culture. It would be hard to find a middle-aged ex-shipyard worker at Nissan.

Although no grants are available in Derbyshire, Toyota are heavily influenced by the enthusiasm of the local county council, including the offer of land at a price that is now being investigated by the EC. The move does seem to mark a shift away from assisted areas, though: Toyota officials say that they do not want to be tied by the obligations that the receipt of grants could imply.

Japanese-owned manufacturers in UK

North Wales	9
South Wales	17
South-west	2
South-central and South-east	18
West Midlands	19
East Midlands	16
Yorkshire	3
North-west	9
North-east	19
Scotland	15
Northern Ireland	2
Total	127

Source: *The Independent*, 30 May 1990

The country decision

The decision on which country to enter may be as circumscribed, or as open, as that of the method of expansion, depending upon the dominant motive for that expansion. If there is a need to penetrate behind tariff barriers, such as those consequent on the changes in the European Community in 1992, then the range of possible locations is automatically

Table 4A Country-related location factors for multinational moves

The economy	Sources of capital	Taxation	Input supplies	Labour
1. Size and rate of growth of GNP	1. Availability of local private-sector capital	1. Corporate tax rates	1. Availability of local raw materials, labour	1. Availability of skilled labour
2. Size and rate of growth of population	2. Cost of local borrowing	2. Other taxes (local, sales, payroll, social security, etc).	2. Existence of local supporting industry	2. Availability of semi-skilled and unskilled labour
3. GNP per head and real disposable income per head	3. Local availability of convertible currencies	3. Tax incentives for investment	3. Availability of water, electricity, gas, oil	3. Level of worker productivity
4. Rate of inflation	4. Government investment grants offered	4. Regulations on remittance of profits	4. Cost and reliability of utilities	4. Industrial training and education
5. Stability and convertibility of currency	5. Availability and cost of export financing	5. Joint tax treaties with home country	5. Tariffs or import restrictions, particularly on components	5. Availability of English-speaking managerial, technical and office staff
6. Foreign exchange position	6. Regulations for the repatriation of capital	6. Tax loss carry forward and back	6. Planned development of 1–5	6. Degree of labour's voice in management
7. Balance of payments outlook		7. Taxation of export income and income earned abroad	7. Local technological climate	7. Freedom of hire and fire

8. Relative dependence on imports and exports
9. Existence of a national economic plan
10. Membership of a Common Market or Free Trade area

8. Taxation of foreign employees
9. Accounting conventions for the calculation of corporate taxes
10. Transfer pricing restrictions

8. Availability of local partners

8. Pattern and strength of unionization
9. Degree of labour disruption
10. Local wage and salary rates
11. Compulsory or customary fringe benefits and profit sharing

Source: P.M. Townroe, *Planning Industrial Location*

Table 4B Country-related location factors for multinational moves

Regional policies	Sites	Markets	Legal requirements	Political factors
1. Area controls over industrial development	1. General availability of suitable plant sites	1. Size and rate of growth of market for company product(s)	1. Structure of company law	1. Form of central, provincial and local government
2. Regional tax incentives	2. Cost of suitable land	2. Competition from local firms	2. Corporate investment laws	2. Stability of government
3. Regional investment grants	3. Proximity of possible sites to: supplies, sources of raw materials, customers, export markets	3. State industries as competitors	3. Legal restrictions on 100 per cent foreign ownership	3. Industrial policies of principal political parties
4. Regional payroll taxes or grants	4. Efficiency of existing local transport system	4. Degree of concentration of competition	4. Legal restrictions to engage in certain types of business	4. Special political, ethnical and social problems
5. Advance factories for purchase or lease	5. Facilities to export and import	5. Degree of tariff protection against foreign competitors	5. Laws for the protection of property rights	5. Nationalization policies
6. Area-specific loans or interest relief	6. Regulations over company-owned transport	6. State of distribution and marketing system	6. Local patent security	6. Government attitudes towards private investment

7. Availability of cheap land

8. Special local training programme

9. Local assistance with worker housing

7. Factory construction costs

8. Range and quality of construction companies

9. Pollution controls

10. Land-use planning controls

7. Presence of local market research, advertising and promotional agencies

7. Price, wage and investment controls

8. Laws on monopoly and restrictive practices

9. Need for special permits and franchise

10. Legal restrictions over the employment of foreign nationals

7. Government attitudes towards foreign investment

8. Commercial links with home country

9. Safety of aliens and their dependants

10. Attitudes to business ethics

Source: P.M. Townroe, *Planning Industrial Location*

limited. Similarly, if the need is to move to areas of low labour costs, to be near existing markets, or to produce in certain types and sizes of market area, the range of choice will be constrained. On the other hand the country decision may be governed by a new and wider range of both objective and subjective factors. These could include the possible attitudes of and incentives offered by governments, the treatment of taxes on remitted profits, the overall quality of the labour force, legislation on pollution and health and safety, the physical and social environment for key personnel and their families, etc. Some of the factors involved are listed in Tables 4A and 4B. Clearly, the decision maker ought to consider a wide range of implications, some of which may not be quantifiable in financial terms.

The site decision

Finally, if it is clear that the only viable option is to set up a greenfield site the actual location will need to be selected. At this stage the many factors detailed earlier will need to be reviewed again, together with the range of incentives offered by local, regional and national governments, the pattern of communications, etc. Firms may resort to the formal methods of investment appraisal discussed earlier. Having decided to locate in a given country it becomes easier to list a limited number of possible sites and discuss their individual advantages or disadvantages in financial terms. For each site in one country projections of revenues may be very similar and the dominant factors may come from the cost side, particularly those for labour and transport. Equally, even if it is a question of a takeover, once the country decision has been taken the basic circumstances will be the same for each possible merger partner, so the techniques of investment appraisal may be employed here.

Conclusion

The discussion above has indicated the wide range of problems that must be considered when contemplating the possibility of expanding abroad. These factors are listed and expanded in the tables in the text. It is unlikely that all items listed will be relevant in each case, and there may be other factors not shown in the tables. In addition, it will not be possible for a firm to assign financial costs and benefits to each item concerned. As a consequence it is almost inevitable that the location decision will be made first of all on the basis of a subjective evaluation. A proper investment appraisal may only be applied at a later stage when the boundaries of the decision have been set in place. Even then, subjective factors may tend to dominate.

Indeed, in the modern world where firms increasingly view themselves as players in a massive corporate game, the dominant factor may not be a rational desire to expand production and maximize profits, as standard theory dictates. More and more expansion seems to be dependent upon such statements as 'taking over the XYZ Games Company fits in well with our picture of Giant Games Corporation as part of the world leisure industry'. As such the decision could be said to be based on the objectives of sales growth and the aggrandizement of power, rather than profit maximization. If this is the case, the location decision may not involve proper appraisal techniques. On the other hand, it is easier to make poor decisions, and such decisions could have implications not only for the company but also for the overall structure of the countries in which it locates.

KEY WORDS

Greenfield sites	Discount rate
Investment appraisal	Takeover
Discounting	Merger
Compound interest	Transaction costs
Present value	Linkages

Reading list

Monk, D., 'A regional policy role play', *Economics Association Journal*, Spring 1986 (a role play).

Armstrong, H. and Taylor, J., *Regional Economics*, chaps 5 – 7, Heinemann Educational, 1990.

Coursework topics

Tables 4A and 4B in the text list the many factors that might be important when planning expansion overseas. Theoretically, management may decide on several possible countries or locations, and then consider each of these factors for each location. A problem then arises in that a monetary or a subjective valuation has to be placed on each item before they can all be added together and the locations ranked in order of preference.

1. Look through the lists and make sure that you understand each item.
2. What would be the most important, and least important, factors in the following cases:

   - a 'colonial' company developing a new tin mine;
   - a UK manufacturer of speciality chemicals expanding overseas;
   - a Japanese producer of consumer goods wishing to expand in Europe;

- a United States conglomerate pursuing a 'global' strategy?

3. Which factors could be quantified? How would you try to add the unquantifiable factors together?

Essay topics

1. What options are available to companies wishing to expand overseas, and how might they choose between these options?
2. What have been the dominant factors leading Japanese firms to invest in the United Kingdom in the latter part of the twentieth century?
3. What economic factors might a major international car manufacturing company take into account when deciding whether to invest £500 million in a new car plant within the UK? (Associated Examining Board, 1990)

Data Response Question 4
Selecting a location within a country
In the passage reproduced on pages 34 and 35, D. Bowen 'looks behind the myths and stereotypes at the reality of UK investment from the Far East' (*The Independent*, 30 May 1990). Read the passage and then answer the following questions.

1. Explain the terms 'the City', 'recruit in the same pool', 'regional grants', 'new towns', and 'assisted areas'.
2. What are the main factors that have attracted Japanese companies to particular regions of the United Kingdom?
3. In what respects is the information given in the text and the accompanying table an inadequate basis from which to judge the impact of Japanese investment on the United Kingdom economy?

Data Response Question 5
Factors influencing location
Our discussion in the text has implied that multinational companies tend to be in manufacturing and concerned only with the location of factories. In the modern world this is less and less the case, as the following article, written by Paul Abrahams and appearing in the *Financial Times* of 5 June 1990, indicates. Based on research work undertaken by Professor Dunning of the University of Reading, it concentrates on the location determinants for multinationals' regional and branch offices. Read the passage and look at the table. Then answer the questions that follow.

1. What is meant by the terms 'just-in-time inventories', and 'integrate their manufacturing operations' in the last paragraph?
2. Use the information in the passage to estimate a suitable number on the scale 0–5 for a sixth factor, 'MARKETS'. Now calculate the *average* factor for each of the six major categories and reconsider the relative importance of the factors, and the commentary of the text. What does this imply for the analysis of the data from such a questionnaire?
3. What does the argument of the passage imply for (i) the implied opportunity cost of executives' time, (ii) the extent to which firms profit-maximize?

Look for a fast road near regular flights

WHY THEY CHOOSE THE UK: on a scale of 0–5
Factors influencing location of an office in the UK
mid-1980s: data from 83 respondents

	Branch	Regional
Transport & telecommunications		
Airports	2.6	3.5
Postal services	1.8	2.4
Telephone and telex quality	2.3	3.0
Telecommunications costs	1.8	2.5
Manpower costs		
Local professional or technical	1.9	2.3
Local secretarial or clerical	1.6	2.1
Language, social, cultural		
Language	1.5	2.2
Living conditions for expatriates*	1.0	1.5
Business framework		
Level of corporate taxation	1.5	2.2
Availability of Govt. incentives**	1.0	1.5
Accommodation		
Availability of right premises	2.5	2.9
Cost of premises to rent etc.	2.2	2.6

* Housing, entertainment, health care, education
** Grants, tax allowances etc.

Source: Dunning, J. H., *Explaining International Production*, Unwin Hyman, 1988.

The 'hassle factor' is how John Dunning, professor of international business at the University of Reading, explains the importance of airports when businesses choose investment locations.

'The proximity of airports, together with effective and cheap telecommunications, represent key variables for multinationals choosing the country and location of a European headquarters', he says.

'Questions such as these are becoming far more important than traditional determinants such as the quality and price of labour, land prices or manufacturing costs'.

The reason is executives' increasing need to travel – not only between their European headquarters and subsidiary companies elsewhere in Europe, but also back to their company's world base in the US or the Far East.

For most business people, despite the blandishments of club- or first-class, these trips soon lose their glamour.

A study by Professor Dunning of 83 multinationals, which decided to locate either their European headquarters or a branch office in the UK during the mid-1980s, showed that, in choosing a regional headquarters, the most important factor was the need to be near an airport (see the accompanying table).

For branch offices, only proximity to clients, market size and prospects, and language were rated above proximity to airports (John H. Dunning, Explaining International Production, Unwin Hyman, 1988).

For manufacturing companies, airports have not historically been as crucial, admits Professor Dunning. However, he believes that, as companies integrate their manufacturing operations and turn increasingly to just-in-time inventories, easy and regular access to air cargo operations will become more important.

Chapter Four
Macroeconomic effects of multinational firms

'The evaluation of the economic costs and benefits of multinational corpo-rations raises many methodological* problems, and conclusions often depend on the assumptions made regarding alternative ways of action', United Nations, *Multinational Corporations in World Development,* 1973 (* refers to methods of analysis used)

At the macroeconomic level much of the argument about multinationals centres on the impact of **foreign direct investment** (FDI). This is the magnitude of investment by firms from one country in the economies of overseas countries. For the UK *inward investment* represents invest-ments by foreign MNEs in the UK economy. Broadly speaking, this can take the form either of investment to finance the purchase of sites, plant and machinery to be used in setting up new subsidiaries (or expanding the operations of existing ones), or in the acquisition of previously British owned companies. On the other hand, *outward FDI* reflects investment by UK-owned MNEs in overseas economies: again this may be a case of expanding existing operations overseas or opening up new ones either by greenfield investment or by acquisition. As we shall see, the UK is an important source of outward FDI as well as being a signifi-cant host for inward FDI.

Inward investment
Table 5 shows a sort of world league table of countries ranked by the amount of inward FDI they attract from foreign MNEs (and to make the figures comparable, all values have been converted into US dollars). This shows very clearly the success of the UK in attracting direct investment from overseas. The total of nearly $14 billion places this country firmly in second place (behind only the USA). Indeed, when expressed in rela-tive terms (i.e. as a proportion of *gross national product*), inward FDI is even more important to the UK than to the US (1.9 as opposed to 1.2 per cent). By the same token, however, some other countries (Spain, Australia and Belgium) overtake the UK in relative terms, but note that these are each relatively minor actors on the world stage.

Moreover, not only is inward FDI into the UK large in absolute terms, it has also grown dramatically over recent years (being only 0.5 per cent of GDP as recently as 1985). But, as can be seen from the table, this dramatic growth is not confined to the UK: in various other countries the average annual growth has been even more dramatic over recent years.

Table 5 The leading host countries for MNEs: foreign direct investment inflows,1988

Country	Inflow: 1988		annual growth rate
	$bn	% of gnp	1983-88(%)
USA	58.5	1.2	37
UK	13.9	1.9	22
France	8.5	1.0	37
Spain	7.0	2.3	34
Italy	6.8	0.9	42
Australia	5.4	2.6	13
Belgium/Lux	5.1	3.4	32
Canada	3.9	0.9	18
Netherlands	3.6	1.7	21
W. Germany	1.6	0.2	4

Reprinted from *Lloyds Bank Economic Bulletin*, June 1990. Original data sources: *IMF Balance of Payments Statistics* and *World Bank Atlas*

Now, as mentioned, this table refers to the *flows* of new investment in a given year, 1988. Another measure of the magnitude of foreign capital in different countries is the *stock* of foreign-owned assets (the stock is merely the sum total of all present and previous investments, allowing for depreciation). Separate data on this measure (not shown in the table) confirms the importance of foreign MNEs within this country. They also reveal that nearly half of all foreign-owned assets in the UK are accounted for by US multinationals (firms such as Ford, General Motors, Esso, Heinz, and Hoover).

Holland is the next most important investor in the UK with 15per cent of all foreign assets (firms such as Unilever, Shell and Philips). The others include Switzerland with 7 per cent (e.g. Nestlé), Canada 5 per cent (e.g. Massey Ferguson), France 4 per cent (e.g. Michelin and Peugeot). Perhaps a little surprisingly, neither of the two economic superpowers, Japan and Germany, accounts for more than 4 per cent of all foreign-owned assets in the UK, although the Japanese share is rising rapidly at the time of writing.

Outward investment

Impressive though the magnitude of investment by foreign firms in the UK is, investment in the opposite direction, by UK firms overseas, is even more substantial, amounting to £20 billion in 1989, which is equivalent to about 3 per cent of GDP. Again, the UK ranks as second only to the US in the world league table. Table 6 shows how the *stock* of overseas assets within the world is split between countries. For the UK these have been estimated at $94 billion by the end of 1987, which amounts to nearly 15 per cent of the world total. It should be noted again how the German and Japanese shares are relatively small, but nevertheless significantly greater than their shares in the UK. Evidently, the Japanese and Germans have not seen the UK as a prime location for their overseas investments in the past, although as just mentioned, there is growing evidence that this is changing as far as the Japanese are concerned.

The effect on the balance of payments

The most obvious and immediate effects of FDI on the macroeconomy are via the **balance of payments**. As the explanation of this is fairly technical, it will help if we first briefly describe what the balance of payments consists of. Table 7 reproduces in summary form the UK balance of payments account for 1989.

This country's dealings with the rest of the world are split into two broad categories. The **current account** includes our (i) visible trade (exports and imports of goods), (ii) invisible trade (exports and imports of services), (iii) interest, dividends and profits paid on investments. As will be seen from Table 7, there is also a fourth item, referring to transfers and grants: this reflects mainly grants to and from foreign countries (i.e. foreign aid) and organizations (e.g. contributions to the EC). For the sake of brevity we shall largely ignore this last category in this discussion. In each category credits refer to money coming into the UK: for sales of exports, and interest, dividends and profits on UK loans and investments overseas. Debits refer to money going out of the UK for purchases of imports and to pay interest, dividends and profits to foreigners on their investments in this country.

The **capital account** represents flows of money into and out of the country for 'transactions in assets and liabilities.' This is where FDI appears under the heading 'Direct investment'. Other categories refer to the purchase and sale of government and company stocks and shares (portfolio investment); borrowing and lending by banks, governments and individuals; and changes in the official reserves of gold and foreign currencies. Entries in the first column refer to investments and loans made by UK firms and individuals and they are shown as negative

Table 6 The leading sources of MNEs:
stock of direct foreign investment by major country of origin, 1985

Country of origin	Share of world total, 1985 (%)
USA	35.1
UK	14.7
Japan	11.7
West Germany	8.4
Switzerland	6.3
Netherlands	6.1
Canada	5.1
France	3.0
Rest of World	8.4
Total	100.0

Source: UN Centre on Transnational Corporations

because they correspond to flows of currency out of the UK, which have a detrimental effect on the balance. Entries in the second column are positive since investments and loans by foreigners into the UK involve inward currency flows.

A last technical point is that, in principle, the capital account should always record a surplus identical to the current account deficit. This is because current account deficits are financed from borrowing and/or the reserves. In fact, owing to errors in statistics and failure to record all transactions, there is always also a residual 'balancing item'.

Now 1989 was a particularly bad year for the UK on the current account. From the table we see that imports of goods exceeded exports by £23.1 billion, and this adverse **balance of trade** was only slightly off-set by surpluses on invisible trade of £4 billion and £4.6 billion on dividends, interest and profits on investments. As there was also a nega-tive balance on the transfers category of £4.6 billion, the overall current account was in deficit to the tune of £19 billion. On the capital account, the UK was a net borrower (partly to pay for the current deficit); but the present estimate of the balancing item suggests that some of these figures are subject to considerable error.

Against this background, we can break down the overall effects of FDI into three parts, two of which appear explicitly, and the third implicitly in the accounts.

1. Effects of initial investment flows
The first and immediate effect is shown in the capital account as 'Direct

Table 7 Balance of payments of the United Kingdom in £ billion: 1989

	Credits	Debits
CURRENT ACCOUNT		
Visible trade	92.5	115.6
Services:		
General government	0.4	2.6
Sea transport	4.0	4.5
Civil aviation	3.8	4.2
Travel (including tourist travel)	6.9	9.3
Financial and other services	15.4	5.9
Total services	30.5	26.5
Interest, profits and dividends		
Direct investments	16.3	9.1
Portfolio investments	7.2	5.7
Other lending by banks	44.7	50.1
Other deposits by other residents	3.9	4.0
Official reserves	1.9	-
Earnings on other assets of government	0.0	0.6
Total interest, profits and dividends	74.0	69.4
Transfers		
Private	1.8	2.1
General government	2.1	6.4
Total current account	200.9	220.0
CAPITAL ACCOUNT		
Direct investment-19.3	+19.6	
Portfolio investment	-37.0	+9.4
Other lending by banks	-27.3	+43.1
Other deposits by other residents	-5.4	+14.9
Other official reserves	+5.4	-
Other government -	0.9	+1.4
Total capital account	-84.4	+88.5
Balancing item		+15

Note: On the capital account a negative sign indicates an increase in UK-owned assets overseas, and therefore an outflow of currency. A plus sign indicates an increase in foreign-owned assets in the UK, and thus an inflow of currency.

Source: *Economic Trends*, July 1990, HMSO.

investment'. This arises because the FDI investments involve flows of currency: outward direct investment by UK firms is an immediate drain on the balance of payments because investment overseas is financed by selling sterling to buy the foreign currency of the countries concerned. Thus, outward FDI from the UK currently runs at £19.3 billion per year and this has the same effect on the external account as would imports of that magnitude. On the other side, inward investment into the UK is financed by foreign companies buying sterling with their own currencies, and this corresponds to an immediate improvement in the external balance. In 1989 this amounted to £19.6 billion, so the net effect was almost zero. However, 1989 was an exceptional year in this respect. Historically, inward investment has been considerably smaller than outward, roughly only half as much in most years. Therefore, usually, the immediate effect of FDI is a net drain on the overall balance (and thus equivalent to a significant excess of imports over exports). The major reason for 1989 being an exception appears to have been the surge of recent takeovers of UK firms by foreign MNEs. We cannot tell yet whether this will be replicated in future years. It is always dangerous to take one year's figure in isolation. But our best bet is that 1989 is an exception which will not be repeated – at least, not at this very high level.

2. Effects of the returns to FDI

We have stressed that the above is the *immediate* effect of FDI. As with all investments, there is a return to be had: in this case, overseas investments will eventually earn profits, resulting in a flow of currency back to the home economy (equivalent to increased exports) of the MNE. This will appear under 'Interest, profits and dividends' relating to 'Direct investments' in the current account. In 1989, as shown in the table, past investments of UK firms overseas yielded a return of £16.3 billion, while past investments by foreign firms in the UK earned them a smaller return (outflow of currency) of £9.1 billion. So on this basis there was a positive effect on the balance of payments of £7.2 billion.

Bringing these effects together, the overall effect on the balance of payments was +£7.4 billion. But because the 1989 inward flow of direct investment was so exceptional this gives a rather false impression. A more representative picture is revealed by repeating the calculations for each of the years in the 1980s (not shown in the table) and then taking the average. We find that, typically, outward investment *exceeded* inward by about £5 billion, while profits, interest and dividends from past outward investment exceeded those on inward investment by about £4 billion.

In other words, in the 'typical' year in the 1980s, UK firms were accumulating investments overseas more rapidly than were foreign firms in the UK, and this had a detrimental effect on the balance of payments. However, this effect was largely cancelled out by the fact that they were receiving greater returns on previous investments than were foreign firms in this country; and this left a net effect of only about £1 billion per year.

We should also add that, in return for this cost, UK companies have been accumulating overseas assets at a much faster rate than are their foreign counterparts in the UK, and this will have beneficial effects on our economy in the future.

3. Effects on trade flows

So far we have discussed only the direct and obvious effects on the balance of payments – those which can be readily seen in the country's published external accounts. However, there are a number of other effects working through the flows of goods and services (i.e. exports and imports). Although less direct and much more difficult to quantify, these are probably equally, if not more, important than those just mentioned.

The most immediate of these again occurs at the time of the initial investment. When a company invests overseas it will install plant and machinery, some of which will probably be imported from its home country; for example, much of the cost of setting up a Japanese car plant in the UK will involve the purchase of Japanese robots, machine tools etc. This will counteract in part the positive influence of the FDI on the balance of payments of the host country.

A second effect can be identified by recalling Figure 1 in Chapter 2, which analysed the choice for a firm between overseas production and exporting. In many instances firms opt for overseas production after having first exported to the market concerned. It follows that as, say, British firms build up their overseas production, they will correspondingly reduce their exports – and the contrary is true for overseas firms operating in the UK. This may be offset to some extent if the multinational firms continue to buy their intermediate products and/or capital equipment from their home country. To cite an example, suppose a UK clothing manufacturer currently exports clothing to the French market. If it now decides to build a plant in France, or to acquire an existing French clothing manufacturer, this will inevitably displace its previous exports to France. If so, while the move to overseas production presumably benefits the UK firm, it harms the UK balance of trade – at least in the short run. These effects are lessened if the UK firm continues to buy its fabrics from UK suppliers (perhaps its own fabrics subsidiaries if it is vertically integrated), but one would still expect a net adverse effect on the UK's balance of trade.

In fact, the chain of events may not stop there. Suppose now that the UK multinational chooses to use its French plant not only to supply its French customers, but also those in adjacent countries. Where this happens, we see a displacement of exports from the firm's original UK plant not only to France, but to other countries as well.

We are now in a position to draw together the various strands of the argument. As a way of summarizing, consider the example of Nissan establishing a car plant in the UK. The initial investment (i.e. purchase of land, capital equipment and buildings) requires a flow of investment into the UK – yen are sold for pounds, and the UK balance of payments improves. In future years, this plant will earn profits, and some of those profits (if they are not reinvested in the UK) will be sent back to Japan. So in the future these will constitute a drain on the UK balance of payments. The effects on trade are as follows. If some of the initial investment requires the purchase of inputs from Japan, the initial inflow of currency will be lessened, but not completely offset. As production from the British plant builds up, Nissan will need to export fewer cars to the UK. Equally if, as promised, ultimately less than 20 per cent of the value of the cars produced are accounted for by Japanese components, this will also improve the UK balance of trade over time. Eventually, it is hoped that the British plant will export Nissan cars to other countries within the EC. To the extent this happens, UK exports are boosted further – at the expense of Japanese exports.

There is no doubt, then, that multinational operations do have important effects on the direction and magnitudes of foreign trade but, as suggested, these are extremely difficult to quantify. The key question is, how do we establish what *would* happen if multinational operation was not an available option for the firms concerned? What *would* exports and imports then look like? Obviously this is an hypothetical question, but one which needs to be faced rather than simply ignored.

The effects on investment and employment

Another major effect claimed for MNEs is on the level of investment in physical plant and machinery. The critics suggest that by choosing to produce overseas, rather than exporting from their own country, UK multinationals are merely investing overseas at the expense of investing at home. If so, the UK economy loses out in two ways. First, it loses the jobs which would have otherwise been created for the new plants here – this is sometimes known rather confusingly as MNEs exporting jobs. Second, assuming that the new investment will be in the latest technology, high-productivity techniques, it is the overseas host, rather than the

UK, which is benefiting from technical progress.

Although this sort of argument is hotly disputed, the sheer scale of overseas investment by UK multinationals dictates that we take it seriously. As mentioned already, the annual outflow of FDI is currently £19 billion, and this amounts to roughly 20 per cent of all UK financed investments. If this were somehow diverted into the UK economy it would undoubtedly dramatically enhance the productive capacity and efficiency of the UK economy. But the acid question is *what would happen if UK firms were somehow prevented from investing overseas?* It is certainly facile to assume that all this extra investment would be automatically switched into productive resources in the home economy. After all, UK firms choose to invest overseas presumably because they assess the likely returns to be higher than from expanding their home operations. It may be that there is just not the range of profitable opportunities available within the home economy – at least for UK multinationals, given the nature of their specific advantages.

Switching the focus to the effects of foreign MNEs investing in the UK, things are even more complicated. Again, at first sight, inward investment is a significant part of total UK investment and we should expect this to have employment enhancing effects as well as helping introduce high-productivity techniques into our economy. One estimate of the effects of inward FDI suggests that it has led to the creation of over 200,000 jobs since 1980 (The Invest in Britain Bureau). This favourable view of foreign MNEs seems to be accepted by governments around the world, as they compete with each other to attract inward investment.

But as always with economics, things are not so simple as that! Expansion by foreign firms will often be at the expense of domestic British firms, so as investment and employment grows in the former, it declines in the latter. This in itself is not a bad thing: if the market economy is to perform efficiently it is inevitable that the efficient should gain at the expense of the inefficient. If domestic UK firms lose out in this competitive race, this is presumably because they are less efficient. But it does suggest that we take with 'a pinch of salt' estimates of the investment and employment enhancing effects of FDI based solely on the direct effects of the foreign MNEs – the **displacement effect** should also be reckoned with.

It is also possible that favourable effects on employment and investment are only real when foreign firms enter the UK by means of greenfield investment. Where entry is effected by means of acquisition of an existing domestic firm much of the investment will relate to the purchase of shares, and there is no certainty of any changed employment effects; indeed, in the short run there are often fears of 'rationalization' and redundancy.

Another criticism of foreign FDI in the UK is that it is pushing us towards the status of a '**screwdriver economy**'. That is, foreign multinationals only choose to site the less technologically advanced stages of their production here, while retaining the more advanced, high-productivity stages for their home economies. This is argued particularly in cases where assembly plants may be located in the UK while the production of the component parts and the background research and development are reserved for their home operations. To the extent that this is true, it means that the UK economy will not necessarily benefit that much from new technology.

Thus far we have talked only of the first-round effects of FDI on investment and employment. Elementary macroeconomic theory alerts us, however, to the consequent **multiplier** effects, which should also be taken into account. Following an initial investment by a foreign firm in the UK there are second-round effects as the firms and individuals who sell to the MNE themselves spend the proceeds and increase demand in the economy further. There follow third, fourth, fifth etc. rounds as the ripple effects of the initial investment work their way through the economy. Again, the effect is opposite for outward investment: if UK firms invest overseas rather than at home these multiplier effects are denied to the UK economy.

But two qualifications must also be made. First, the multiplier effects will be stunted if the economy is already working at full capacity: the extra demands on goods and services will not then lead to increased real activity but merely to higher prices, as demand will have increased while supply has remained constant. This suggests that the relative merits of FDI should always be judged taking into account the current state of demand in the home economy.

The second qualification concerns the relative magnitudes and leakages of multipliers associated with different types of investment. In standard macroeconomics textbook explanations it is convenient to talk about 'the multiplier' as if there is a given magnitude which applies to all investments. While this is acceptable in a textbook designed to convey a relatively complex idea in simple terms, it is hardly appropriate in the real world. In practice, different types of investment will exhibit different multipliers. To explain why, remember our earlier discussion about the trade effects of FDI. Suppose, hypothetically, that virtually all the investment of a foreign firm setting up a new plant in the UK is spent on buying in machinery from its home country. In that case there is in effect very little investment in the UK and correspondingly virtually no multiplier effects *within this country*: substantial leakages have led to a very low multiplier. Similarly, if a UK MNE fits up its overseas factories with British machinery there will be a multiplier effect within the UK, even though the investment is physically located overseas. It is for precisely this reason that governments are often anxious to secure promises from foreign MNEs that their investment will involve substantial linkages to the host economy.

KEY WORDS

Foreign direct investment	Capital account
Inward investment	Balance of trade
Outward investment	Displacement effect
Balance of payments	Screwdriver economy
Current account	Multiplier

Reading list:

Anderton, A.G., Work Card 31, 'UK overseas assets and liabilities' in *Data Response Workpack in A-Level Economics*, UTP, 1985.

Bazen, S. and Thirlwall, T., *Deindustrialization*, chap 5, Heinemann Educational, 1989.

Chrystal, K.A., 'Have high capital flows harmed Britain?', *Economic Review*, Sept. 1985.

Eatwell, J., *Whatever Happened to Britain?*, chap 5, Duckworth, 1983.

Essay topics

1. Compare and contrast the macroeconomic effects of a foreign company that invests in the United Kingdom by: (a) setting up a 'greenfield' site operation that depends in part upon imported components, exports half its output, and remits half its profits home; and (b) invests in the United Kingdom by taking over an existing manufacturing company.

2. What might be (a) the short run, and (b) the long run, consequences of a ban on UK firms investing overseas?

3. Assess the possible consequences of the single integrated European market ('1992') for the pattern of multinational operations within the European Community.

Data Response Question 6
Balance of payments effects

Table 7 in the text gives detailed balance of payments statistics for the United Kingdom for 1989. First of all make sure that you understand the meaning of the various headings in the table, in particular, the directions of the currency flows implied by the various items on the current and capital accounts. Then answer the following questions.

1. Which items in the table could have been affected by (a) a United Kingdom company buying an office block in San Francisco, (b) a United States insurance company taking over a United Kingdom insurance company, (c) a Japanese electronics manufacturing company setting up a production branch in the United Kingdom?

2. Which items in the balance of payments statistics for 1991 might be affected by the three transactions referred to in question 1?

3. If, in 1989, a Hong Kong producer had spent £100 million on setting up a greenfield operation in the United Kingdom, expecting that in five years it would reach a £30 million turnover, export half its output, import a tenth of its components, provide a rate of return on capital of 15 per cent, remit three-quarters of its profits home, and employ 300 workers, only 15 of whom would be Hong Kong personnel, what would be its net impact on the balance of payments statistics in 1994?

Chapter Five
The industrial effects of multinationals

'Incoming multinationals are often credited with providing beneficial contributions to Britain in addition to bringing new industries and new technologies. They are seen to create jobs, investment, exports, productivity gains, and other benefits not readily achievable by local firms' J. M. Stopford and L. Turner.

In the previous chapter we concentrated on the consequences of FDI and multinational firms for the macroeconomy. The effects considered, on the balance of trade and payments, investment, and aggregate employment, are usually those which feature most strongly in the popular debate about MNEs. However, as with all macroeconomic issues, our understanding can be enhanced by moving the level of analysis down to microeconomics, to consider the performance of individual firms and industries. Ultimately, the performance of the aggregate UK economy, in terms of trade and growth, will be determined by the performance of its firms on productivity, technical progressiveness and competitiveness. This leads us inevitably to look at the influence of MNEs on the structure and competition within individual industries, and their effects on productivity, wages and technical progress in those industries. That is the subject of this chapter. Here, our emphasis will be on the impact of foreign-owned MNEs on the British economy, with rather less attention placed on the influence of UK-owned multinationals on the microeconomies of their overseas hosts.

The structural distribution of foreign-owned MNEs in the UK

The obvious first step is to establish within which sectors of the UK economy foreign MNEs predominate. This is shown first at the very broad level in Figure 4, which charts the proportions of the total stock of foreign-owned assets (capital) accounted for by firms in each of six sectors of economic activity. As can be seen, manufacturing industries are clearly the most important: over a third of all foreign-owned assets in this country are accounted for by firms in this sector. This result will not be peculiar to the UK; manufacturing is typically the largest sector in most Western nations and it is not surprising to find that it also attracts the

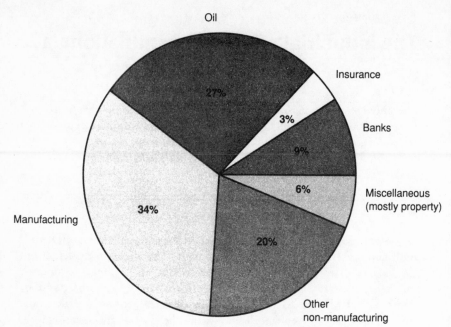

Figure 4 The proportions of foreign owned assets in broad sections of the UK economy.

Source: *Lloyds Bank Economic Bulletin*, June 1990

largest share of inward FDI. The next most important are the oil companies (Esso, Shell, Mobil, Texaco etc.) who account for over a quarter of all foreign assets in the UK. Again, this is not unusual: the oil industry was probably the first truly international industry, with the same small number of oligopolists competing, and therefore locating, in many different national markets around the world. Now, although these two are by far and away the most important sectors for foreign firms in this country, their *share* of the total has actually declined over the last decade (in 1981, for example, manufacturing's share was significantly higher at 41 per cent). This reflects two forces at work.

The first is that manufacturing as a whole has become steadily less important within the UK economy, especially during the period of depressed activity and high unemployment in the first five years of the Thatcher government. It is natural, therefore, that it will have also attracted a declining share of inward FDI in recent years.

The second force reflects the other side of the coin: as manufacturing and, to a lesser extent, oil have become less important in relative terms, the other, service, sectors have become relatively more important. This is especially so for financial services, shown in the figure as banks, insurance and miscellaneous (mostly property) which together account for nearly 20 per cent of all foreign-owned assets. Here, there are a number of noteworthy explanations. The first concerns the nature of services: as a broad generalization, it is true to say that *many services exhibit an income elasticity of demand greater than one*. This means that as incomes rise, demand for those services rises more than proportionately, and they therefore account for an increasing proportion of expenditure (and thus GDP). So as a developed country becomes richer, financial services will become a more important part of the economy, and we should expect all firms, both foreign and home based, to divert more of their resources in that direction.

But also, over the last twenty years financial services have become increasingly worldwide industries. It is noticeable, for example, how many of the impressive buildings in the City of London now house foreign banks and other financial institutions. Undoubtedly the internationalization of industries such as banking, insurance and, to some extent, property reflects the breathtaking advances in recent years in information technology. These points are applicable to most countries, but in the British setting, there was also an additional factor, *financial deregulation*: such major events as 'Competition and Credit Control' in 1971, and more recently, the 'Big Bang' in the City being the most striking examples, both making it easier for foreign banks and other financial institutions to compete in the British marketplace. Finally, the remaining sector in the figure, 'Other non-manu-facturing' is a 'hotchpotch', including construction, mining, distribution, transport and other industries, none of which has a large enough foreign share to merit separate discussion.

We turn now to a slightly different way of looking at the distribution of foreign capital across sectors, and consider the '**penetration rate**' of foreign firms. In other words, in which sectors do foreign firms have the most dominant role (i.e. share of the market). We do this by calculating the proportion of the total assets of each sector that is owned by foreign firms, i.e. the value of foreign assets divided by the total assets of the sector. Looked at in this way, manufacturing is still the leading sector: of the total assets of all 'industrial and commercial' companies in this country, 19 per cent are accounted for by foreign firms. This is a rise from 14 per cent in 1982, so foreign penetration has increased in this sector. However, penetration is nearly as high in banking – 16.5 per cent. But the most striking change in the 1980s has been in the 'other financial institutions': while foreign MNEs accounted for only 3 per cent of their total assets in 1982, this had risen to 10 per cent in 1987. This is undoubtedly the result of the internationalization and deregulation of this sector just mentioned.

The structural distribution of
foreign-owned MNEs in UK manufacturing

Having established the facts at the broad sector level we now consider a more detailed analysis of industries within the manufacturing sector. We concentrate on manufacturing partly because, as just seen, it is the most important sector, but also because official statistics are not collected for individual industries within the other sectors of Figure 4. For this purpose, 'manufacturing' has been split up into 18 'industries', each of which actually represents a number of smaller parts. Thus the first one shown, in Table 8, 'Motor vehicles', refers to lorries, caravans and trailers, and motor components, as well as, most importantly, motor cars. The first column of the table shows, for each industry, the proportion of its output accounted for by the subsidiaries of foreign firms. Thus they account for about 45 per cent of the net output of the UK motor industry, 37 per cent of office machinery, and so on. Running down the 'league table', one is struck by the fact that the top half includes most of the fast-growth and high-technology industries, such as electrical and instrument engineering and office machinery, as well as chemicals and cars. On the other hand, the lower half of the table, in which foreign firms are relatively rare, includes many of the more traditional industries whose products are mature and unlikely to develop much technologically or to face rapid demand growth in the future. Timber, furniture, non-metallic minerals (i.e. bricks, cement etc.) seem to fit this description closely, as do textiles, clothing and leather.

Thus, foreign-owned firms seem to be especially well placed to benefit from industrial growth in the UK over the next few decades. Yet it would be wrong to think of them as having cornered all the promising parts of manufacturing. The foreign share overall is less than 20 per cent, and even in their preferred sectors, the share rarely exceeds one-third. Since this figure has increased only moderately over the last twenty years, and bearing in mind one of the findings of a current research project being undertaken at UEA, namely that over 40 per cent of all UK manufacturing is accounted for by the *home* operations of UK MNEs, these numbers do not reveal an especially dominating role for foreign firms.

Productivity, wages and profitability

The remaining columns of the table take us on to some issues which are at the heart of the debate about the performance of foreign multinationals within UK manufacturing. Are they more productive than domestic UK firms, and, if so, do their workers benefit or is the greater productivity appropriated in the form of higher profits?

Table 8 Foreign multinationals in UK manufacturing

	Share of output (%)	Productivity differential	Wage differential	Profit differential
All manufacturing of which:	17.9	1.34	1.19	1.13
Motor vehicles	44.8	1.20	1.15	1.04
Office machinery	36.6	1.09	1.20	0.91
Chemicals	32.8	1.12	1.05	1.07
Rubber and plastics	23.6	1.25	1.17	1.07
Instrument engineering	22.6	1.09	1.05	1.04
Mechanical engineering	20.1	1.25	1.11	1.13
Electrical engineering	17.2	1.14	1.06	1.08
Paper/Printing/Publishing	15.5	1.22	1.14	1.07
Food/Drink/Tobacco	14.8	1.48	1.15	1.29
Metals manufacture	13.4	1.01	1.05	0.96
Metal goods	11.4	1.34	1.11	1.21
Man made fibres	9.4	0.96	0.95	1.01
Non-metallic minerals	7.6	1.07	0.97	1.10
Textiles	3.9	1.30	1.06	1.23
Clothing/Footwear	3.7	1.11	1.10	1.01
Timber/Furniture	3.2	1.26	1.05	1.20
Other transport equipment	2.1	1.16	1.06	1.09
Leather	1.4	1.12	1.15	0.97

Notes: 'Share of output' shows the percentage of the output of each industry account-ed for by subsidiaries of foreign-owned firms (foreign MNEs). 'Productivity differential' shows the ratio of labour productivity in foreign MNEs to productivity in UK-owned firms in the industry. 'Wage differential' shows the ratio of the average wage paid by foreign MNEs to the average wage paid by UK-owned firms in the industry. 'Profitability differential' shows the ratio of profitability in foreign MNEs to profitability in UK-owned firms in the industry.

Source: *Census of Industrial Production*, HMSO, 1990.

To answer these questions we first require some objective statistical measure of the level of productivity or efficiency in a given firm or industry. There are various ways this can be measured, the most popular being **labour productivity**, defined as the firm's net output divided by the number of workers it employs; that is, the amount of output produced by the average worker. Two words of explanation are called for. First, by looking at *net* output (the value of the firm's sales minus the amount of raw materials and intermediate products used to produce its end product) we are attributing to the employees only the **value added** they produce. (This is to ensure comparability between different types of industry which lie at different stages in the vertical chain of production.) Second, in looking at the productivity of employees we ignore the other factors of production employed, notably capital.

While this is common practice it runs the risk of misleading conclusions about efficiency. For example, workers in firm A may have much larger labour productivity than those in firm B, not necessarily because they are better workers, or because the firm is more efficient, but simply because firm A uses much more capital-intensive methods of production (i.e. a much larger stock of capital equipment). If so, A's **capital productivity** may be lower than B's, and it is debatable whether A is more or less 'efficient' than B. In fact, there are more sophisticated measures of total productivity which we could use which examine the productivity of all factors of production simultaneously. But for our purposes here labour productivity will suffice, so long as it is remembered that a potential cause of higher productivity is greater use of capital equipment.

The second column of the table shows for each industry the productivity differential between foreign-owned firms and domestic firms, i.e. the ratio of average labour productivity in foreign firms to average labour productivity in domestically owned firms. So in manufacturing as a whole with a ratio of 1.34, this means that foreign multinationals have an advantage of 34 per cent: the average worker in a foreign multinational produces over a third more than his/her counterpart in a domestically owned firm. This is very striking evidence that foreign firms are in some way more productive or efficient than domestic firms.

Running down the list of industries it is clear that foreign firms are more productive in virtually all parts of manufacturing, although the exact value of the differential does vary quite considerably. It is particularly high in food, drink and tobacco, metal goods and textiles, but much smaller in office machinery, non-metallic minerals and instrument engineering. In two sectors, metals and man-made fibres, there appears to be no differential of any substance.

Closer inspection of this column reveals what appears at first sight to be a puzzle. In only one individual industry is the differential higher than the overall figure for manufacturing as a whole. This would appear to be nonsensical: usually the average of a series of numbers lies somewhere in the middle, with roughly as many numbers below the average as above it. In fact, there is no error in our calculations, instead this is evidence of a very important phenomenon. The overall average differential is what is known as a *weighted average* and the fact that it is significantly larger than the simple average of the numbers tells us that the productivity differential is highest in those industries which, by their nature, tend to be high-productivity industries. This reveals that there is a tendency for foreign firms to choose to locate themselves in the most productive parts of British industry. Using more advanced statistical techniques, the authors have shown that this *structural* effect accounts for almost exactly half of the overall productivity differential.

Thus we may conclude that, on average, productivity in foreign-owned firms is about 34 per cent higher than in domestically owned firms. This is accounted for partly by a greater congregation of foreign multinationals in high-productivity (i.e. high-technology) industries, and partly because they achieve higher productivity than comparable domestically owned firms.

Turning to the third column of the table, we investigate the corresponding *wage differential*. Again, this is calculated as a ratio: the average wage paid in foreign firms divided by the average wage in domestic firms. There are certainly similarities with the picture for productivity: in manufacturing as a whole, the ratio is higher than one; the average employee of a foreign-owned firm earns 20 per cent more than his/her counterpart in a domestically owned firm; there are significant variations in the differential between industries; and the overall average is larger than in nearly all the individual industries, reflecting a tendency for foreign firms to congregate in high-wage industries. None of this is particularly surprising since one would expect higher wages to go hand in hand with higher productivity: this is certainly consistent with the standard microeconomic theory of factor markets which predicts that workers will be paid a wage equal to their marginal product, which will be related in turn to average productivity.

On the other hand there is one striking difference between the figures in the productivity and wage columns: the former are invariably larger than the latter. This reveals that although foreign firms are more efficient in the sense that their workers typically produce more, not all of the difference is passed on in the form of higher wages. This can only mean that foreign-owned firms are taking part of the higher productivity in the form of higher profits. This is shown in the last column of the table, which reports the values of a third ratio. Very loosely speaking, this reflects the differential between profitability in foreign-owned and domestic firms. Again, the same pattern emerges: the ratio is usually greater than one, it varies significantly between industries, and the overall average is larger than most of the individual industry figures. So foreign firms tend to be more profitable than domestically owned firms (by how much depends on the exact industry being considered) but there is also a tendency for foreign firms to be more numerous in more profitable industries. This is entirely consistent with our suggestion that foreign firms usually employ more capital equipment than domestic ones – the greater profitability then merely reflects the returns to that capital.

Why are foreign multinationals more productive?

We are now in a position to combine some of the above findings with the theoretical discussion in Chapter 2. We saw earlier that it is generally believed that multinationals differ from other firms in possessing some specific advantage – this is the reason why they choose to 'go multinational' in the first place. If so, and particularly if that advantage is technological, it is hardly surprising that they achieve higher productivity levels. In this respect it is significant that the table shows the foreign multinational presence to be particularly high in high-technology industries, typically associated with large R&D (research and development) expenditures.

A second possibility is that multinationals simply employ 'better' factors of production. In part this is the specific asset argument in a different guise; that is, these firms have superior management and/or management techniques, and organize work practices for the labour force more efficiently. But also it may be to do with better training of the workforce, and possibly the ability to employ harder working or more able workers. This is certainly consistent with the evidence on the higher wages that they employ.

A third possibility was raised earlier. It may be that foreign multinationals invest more heavily in capital equipment. Thus their workers have access to more mechanized methods of production, and this is the reason why they are more productive. Now this may be evidence of greater efficiency, and it is certainly widely believed that greater capital intensity is 'a good thing' and is indicative of greater efficiency. However, there is a sense in which firms may be 'too capital intensive'. This occurs where they could produce the same output with less capital, and more labour, more cheaply. Both from the point of view of the firm and society it is generally preferable that the *least-cost* methods of production should be employed. These will not always be the most capital intensive – it depends on the relative prices of labour and capital. This is not to suggest necessarily that foreign multinationals *are* too capital intensive, only that this cannot be ruled out as a possibility, and that, strictly speaking, higher labour productivity is not necessarily evidence of greater efficiency. Having said this, the results of this section are certainly suggestive that foreign multinationals in the UK context do tend to be more efficient.

Concentration and market power

Thus far all the evidence seems to point in favour of multinationals. But as suggested earlier, worries are sometimes expressed that they are usually large firms with dominant positions in the industries in which they operate. As such they may exploit their market power by charging high prices to consumers.

This is a difficult hypothesis to test directly. There have undoubtedly been individual cases where proposed takeovers by multinationals have attracted the attention of the Monopolies and Mergers Commission, because it was feared that this might lead to 'too much' market power.

It is also true that multinationals *are* often in powerful positions within individual industries. Household names such as Ford, Unilever, the big oil companies, Michelin, Hoover, IBM, Heinz, Kelloggs and so on easily come to mind. We have also undertaken a more systematic study in which we investigated the market shares of the five leading firms in each of 140 industries within manufacturing (included under the broad categories already listed in the table). That investigation showed that just over 422 firms held these leading positions (note that this is considerably less than the 700 implied by multiplying 5 by 140, because many firms are diversified and in leading positions in more than one industry). Of those 422 firms, as many as one-third were foreign multinationals. Since this proportion is much higher than the multinational share of total manufacturing output shown in the table, we can conclude that there is a tendency for these firms to have an importance rather greater than the 20 per cent earlier identified. Indeed in a dozen or so highly concentrated individual industries, virtually all the leading positions were held by multinationals.

Given the lack of extensive direct research findings currently available on the market power exhibited by multinationals in the UK, our conclusion must be left open. But there *are* theoretical grounds for viewing market power with suspicion, and this should be borne in mind before accepting the otherwise generally favourable conclusions to be drawn from the evidence of this chapter.

KEY WORDS

Penetration rate	Value added
Labour productivity	Capital productivity

Reading list

Bazen, S. and Thirlwall, T., *Deindustrialization*, chap. 4, Heinemann Educational, 1989.

Eatwell, J., *Whatever Happened to Britain?*, chap. 7, Duckworth, 1983.

R., Levačić, *Supply Side Economics*, chap. 2, Heinemann Educational, 1988.

Essay topics

1. Examine the possible microeconomic effects of a French company (a) taking over a major local company in your area, or (b) setting up a local rival to your major local company. Which do you think would have the better results for your local economy, and why?

2. Does the steady growth in the operations of multinational companies necessarily lead to increased competition, or to increased concentration, in industrial countries' markets?

3. To what extent does the advance of technology, and the steady increase in economies of scale, necessitate the further globalization of manufacturing industry?

4. How would you compare the size of firms? Account for the simultaneous existence of firms of different size within the same industry. Explain and comment on the link between the size of firms within an industry and the competitiveness of that industry. (University of Cambridge Local Examinations Syndicate, 1988).

5. Why might foreign multinationals employ better trained workers than indigenous firms?

Data Response Question 7

Foreign ownership, concentration and productivity

Study the data in Table 9 below, derived from the Census of Production for 1987, published by the Business Statistics Office, and then answer the following questions.

1. Using the data for all firms, rank the industries by size according to the four variables given in the table. Why do the rankings differ?

2. Using the percentage data for foreign firms, and for the largest four firms, rank the industries by concentration and by strength of foreign ownership. Is there any evidence that foreign firms tend to be located in the most concentrated industries?

3. Use the data to assess whether foreign firms tend to have higher sales per employee, and more capital expenditure per unit of output, than either all firms or the largest four firms.

Table 9 Selected UK manufacturing industries: 1987

Industry	All firms			
	Firms	Employment	Gross output	Net capital expend
		(000s)	(£bn)	(£mn)
31 Metal goods not elsewhere specified	13 437	316.1	11.3	406.8
34 Electrical and electronic engineering	9 295	544.9	22.2	836.2
35 Motor vehicles & parts	1 945	258.0	17.6	611.7
37 Instrument engineering	2 525	83.2	2.9	113.7
43 Textiles	4 378	228.1	7.6	271.4
47 Paper, printing & publishing	21 011	446.1	21.9	1 069.6

(a) and (b) As percentage of the totals for all firms

Industry	(a) Foreign-owned firms				(b) Largest four firms			
	Firms	Employment	Gross output	Net capital expend	Firms	Employment	Gross output	Net capital expend
31	0.8	7.9	12.5	13.2	0.0	6.4	9.1	9.1
34	2.3	16.1	21.6	23.6	0.0	27.5	26.1	21.7
35	2.5	31.6	49.1	42.9	0.2	44.1	60.0	68.0
37	3.2	20.7	26.6	23.2	0.2	10.1	10.6	14.0
43	0.7	3.2	5.3	3.9	0.1	20.8	19.8	17.3
47	0.8	11.4	16.2	17.3	0.0	10.6	11.3	11.4

Data Response Question 8
Foreign ownership and market structure

The passage on page 68 is taken from an academic article on 'Foreign ownership and market structure in the United Kingdom' by Steven Globerman, published in *Applied Economics* in 1979. Read the passage and then answer the questions below.

1. Explain the terms 'oligopolistic', 'entry barriers' and 'above normal profits'.
2. Explain the argument of the passage in your own words.
3. What are the implications for government policy, if multinational firms are heavily concentrated in oligopolistic industries?

Market structure and international production

One set of hypotheses maintains that direct investment is an instrument for restraining competition between firms of different nations. One version of the relationship suggests that oligopolistic multinational firms seek to extend their market power in host countries by acquiring domestically-owned firms, thereby reducing the number of independent competitors in domestic markets. The long-run expected benefits of reducing competition through acquisitions of domestically-owned firms will be positively related to industry entry barriers. More specifically, above normal profits resulting from initial reductions in the number of independent competitors will be competed away if new domestic firms can easily enter an industry. To the extent that industrial concentration serves as a summary measure of barriers to entry, the 'restraint of competition' hypothesis provides a basis for expecting foreign ownership and industrial concentration to be positively related. The long-run expected benefits of reducing competition fortify the existing market shares of established firms. This may be especially the case in oligopolistic industries in which firms compete primarily by attempting to create brand loyalty. This motive also presumes that direct investment can permanently alter market structure conditions in an industry.

Chapter Six

Government attitudes to multinationals

'The Government is committed to maintaining a business environment which has allowed the UK to achieve its leading position as an investment location'. Douglas Hogg, QC, MP, Minister for Industry and Enterprise, in the Annual Report 1989/90 of the Invest in Britain Bureau

Why welcome multinationals?

Previous chapters have discussed the theory and evidence on a number of effects of multinational firms, varying from their impact on the balance of payments to their implications for the structure of individual industries. Not all of these effects were positive, so why then do most countries follow the sentiments expressed in the quotation above, and actively welcome and entice overseas firms to set up operations in their countries?

Balancing the specific effects

Let us start by reviewing the effects discussed in previous chapters. In doing so we should bear in mind that the firm could be a UK organization beginning to produce abroad, or it could be a foreign corporation entering the United Kingdom. Again, the firm could be setting up a greenfield site, or it could be engaging in a takeover bid for a domestic company.

The effects we have already discussed include: on the balance of payments, fairly immediate impacts on the capital account, and changes in current account flows of interest, profits and dividends, and exports and imports of goods and services, extended over time. On the industrial side there will be immediate effects resulting from the purchase of capital goods and the erection of buildings, with consequent multiplier spin-offs. There will be on-going employment effects, together with the need for increased outputs by sub-contractors and suppliers. Transport demands may add to congestion. In the long run there will perhaps be a boost to training and the production of a skilled work-force, and an improvement in the technological base. On the other hand there may be long-run implications for the level of competition in the home industry.

Appraisal methods

If government were to assess each proposal by a foreign multinational company to start production in the United Kingdom, then the effects noted above would need to be taken into account. The obvious procedure would be to list them under two headings, 'good' and 'bad', and then quantify one list against the other. This would be complicated because, on the one hand, the effects take place at different periods of time, so that time profiles of each would be needed, and, on the other hand, it is not at all clear that all factors can be quantified financially. It may be possible to calculate the net impact on employment, but assessment of the eventual impact on industrial structure and competitiveness will be very difficult. If all the effects *could* be quantified, then the evaluation process would be essentially similar to the process of investment appraisal described in Chapter 3.

However, there is a difference. Normal investment appraisal techniques are designed for use by profit-maximizing firms. They require estimates of the financial costs of a project, and the net revenues gained from pursuing it, but *only* the costs and revenues borne and received by the firm. They will not include **external costs and benefits** borne by the community at large, such as the costs of counteracting pollution, or the benefits of a general improvement in workforce skills. Consequently, standard investment appraisal techniques are inappropriate for use by government, which ought to be maximizing the overall welfare of the nation at large and not just the welfare of one firm.

Instead the appropriate appraisal technique for government is **cost–benefit analysis**. In a cost–benefit analysis the value of all the costs and benefits of a proposed project are taken into account, so that the sum relates to society as a whole. Then, just as in techniques of investment appraisal, the flow of costs and benefits over time is discounted using appropriate discount rates. Applying cost–benefit appraisal to the plans of a multinational company setting up a greenfield operation in the United Kingdom could include costs such as those of additional traffic congestion or pollution. Benefits might include the effective reduction in unemployment (allowing for multiplier effects), the net impact on the balance of payments etc.

Undertaking such a calculation in monetary terms would be very difficult. It would need a team of economists to try to estimate, for example, the costs imposed on other lorry drivers by having an additional stream of lorries occupying a given road space. However, such calculations are already undertaken for major infrastructure projects such as the construction of a third London airport, and they could be done to assess the value of a multinational company commencing production in the United Kingdom. However, in this day and age, not only would the monetary evaluation of all factors be *difficult*, it might even be considered *inappropriate* by the government. Political considerations might dominate the monetary evaluation. For example, a project that reduces unemployment in the North East region may be valued much more highly than one that has a similar effect elsewhere. A project that might quickly reduce imports could be valued more highly than another that might have a larger impact, in the long run, on increasing exports. Thus, the application of politically-biased weights to specific factors might rank projects in ways totally at variance with those produced by a purely monetary cost–benefit analysis.

Why do governments enthuse over multinationals?

The implications of this discussion are that it is quite possible that the negative factors could outweigh the positive ones, and that sometimes the project should be denied. Yet, as the quotation at the start of the chapter indicates, governments normally fall over backwards trying to attract foreign investment to their shores. Why are they so enthusiastic?

The root cause probably lies in the arguments about why firms go multinational in the first place, discussed in Chapter 2. Almost certainly, in government eyes, multinational firms are those that have specific advantages in one or other fields. They are normally large in size and already efficient operators in their home markets. They are likely to have particular technological advantages in their products, and be efficient in their production methods. If you can attract a wide range of multinational operations to your country you increase the overall productivity and technological sophistication of your economy. More-over, you do it in a relatively painless manner. It occurs without any need to subsidize research and development, train workers, or bribe home companies to invest.

Beyond this, there is a problem of competitiveness. If country A does not acquire Optimal Ozone Plc, then country B will. Far better to have Nissan producing cars in the United Kingdom, and exporting them to the EC, than have them produce in France and let the UK import cars. If the supply of mobile international industry is restricted then governments will vie with one another to attract multinational firms to their country rather than see them go elsewhere.

Thus, by and large governments are enthusiastic about multinational firms because they are the easy option. Governments tend to discount any disadvantages that might arise, and they certainly do not want an innovative, employment-creating company to site itself in a nearby competitive nation.

The question begged

But if this is the case, does this not reveal something about the economy of the host country? Why should the United Kingdom go out of its way to entice Nissan or Toyota to produce cars in the UK when it has its 'own' car industry? Could not the British firms expand instead? Is it really necessary that in computers, ICL should be taken over by Fujitsu? Does not the enthusiasm for overseas multinationals stem really from inherent weakness in the home economy? Is it not merely another way of saying 'We as a nation are technologically inept, so let us welcome as many outsiders as possible'.

This is certainly a possible view to take. One can point to considerable areas of United Kingdom industry that are not very efficient or competitive in international terms. In these circumstances, anything that improves productivity and efficiency is to be welcomed. Moreover, if one recalls the theory of comparative advantage, and adds to that theory the conditions of modern technological industry, then government enthusiasm for multinationals becomes even more understandable. In the modern world economies of scale may set in at transnational volumes, and they may apply to the introduction of new products, the extent of research and development, the sophistication of marketing etc. In these circumstances no medium or small country can hope to have a comparative advantage in even a sizable fraction of the whole range of modern goods and services. All it can hope is to be good in a restricted range of commodities. Then the encouragement of multinationals to produce in your country becomes a method of extending the range of your comparative advantage, as well as increasing your overall productivity and standard of living. The root cause is again the specific advantages held by the multinational firms.

Problems for government; the role of organization structure

Nevertheless there are some issues on which governments voice concern. A number of these problems are associated with the organizational nature of the activity undertaken in the host country, and this is discussed first.

If you consider a normal United Kingdom company of modest to large size, its organizational structure comprises a head office unit and a number of factory locations. The head office will be concerned largely with administrative and professional activities, such as finance, personnel, marketing etc. A large part of these activities will be directed towards keeping the company growing and profitable over the long term. They will be concerned with product planning, research and development, strategy over mergers and takeovers etc. A further element in long-term development will be the establishment of a research and development unit, which may be attached to a factory but also could occupy a self-standing location. The other role of the head office is, of course, to oversee the day to day operations of the company, but the actual operations are carried out at the factories. These may have a very limited long-term decision-making role. They simply produce and distribute the products.

When a multinational company sets up in a host country, it is almost always simply a factory unit, the 'branch plant', rarely involving any long-term decision-making capability. Research and development, product planning and development, financial strategy, all remain in the company's head office overseas. The host country acquires an up-to-date production unit, but not a long-term decision-making capability. The same situation may occur with a takeover. The multinational may withdraw the decision-making capability from the United Kingdom back to its home base, leaving the UK firm merely as a productive shell. Control of the company's destiny has been lost to another country.

With this background we can now consider some of the problems that multinational companies pose for governments. These include problems associated with profits transmission, branch plants and regional problems, the maintenance of competition and the use and abuse of power.

Profits and their transmission

Firms become multinationals partly to increase their overall profits. Their shareholders will be located mainly in the home country. Naturally, there is a requirement that the operations overseas should remit all the profits back home. Consequently, if one compares two identical plants, one home-owned and one owned by a multinational, two problems arise. First, the remission of profits produces a drain on the host country's balance of payments. For most developed countries this is not a serious matter as they also acquire an inward flow of profits and dividends from the investments by their own multinational firms overseas; but for less-developed countries a steady outward stream of remitted profits might be very unwelcome. Secondly, whereas the home company would, in part, use profits to finance new investment and expansion, for the multinational, all such decisions are made in its own head office, back in its own country of origin. Hence, profits made by the UK branch plant could be entirely used to finance investment in a plant in West Germany. The control of the domestic plant's destiny has been lost.

The situation can be worse than this. Suppose that a multinational company has plants in several countries and they make a variety of components that are exported from one plant to another, with one plant producing the finished product. Further suppose that the rates of corporation tax in each country differ. By operating a process known as **transfer pricing** the multinational can operate so as to minimize the amount of tax it pays, and maximize the amount of profit that it retains. Of course, for the company this is splendid, but it may not be welcome news to the governments of countries that are trying to balance their budgets by obtaining tax revenue from companies.

To understand the principle of transfer pricing a simple example will suffice. A multinational company produces a component in country A and exports it to its plant in country B, where it is incorporated in the finished product. It makes one million components a year and they cost £1 to produce. The factory in A will have to produce its accounts every year, and it will have to pay corporation tax according to the law of country A. This will apply similarly to B. In addition, to export the commodity from A to B a price will be have to be quoted so that the commodity is valued for balance of payments purposes. As the sale is actually internal to the firm, even though it is between two countries, the price set is an internal price, not a market price, and the firm can set any price it likes. This is the transfer price, the price at which the component is transferred within the firm.

Suppose now that two countries have different tax regimes but market conditions dictate that the price of the final product is £50. Also assume that without any addition due to the transfer price the total cost of production is £46, so that the maximum possible profit per unit is £4. If country A has a very low rate of tax and country B has a high rate of tax, then it will pay the firm to make as much profit as possible in A, and make very little in B. To do this it sets a high transfer price on the component, say £5, so that it makes £4 profit per unit in A. On the other hand profitability in B will be zero as it appears to buy in the £1 component at £5, so that its total costs now appear at £50, which is exactly the market price. If the tax regimes were to be reversed the company would simply shift the transfer price down towards the original cost of £1, thereby making very little profit in country A, but reveal total costs of £46 in country B, in which it is now making high profits. Note that for transfer pricing to be totally successful it is not only necessary that the tax regimes should differ. It is also necessary that firms should be able to remit profits out of the country. It is no use making vast profits in Outer Mongolia if you cannot get them out, there is nothing to do with them there, and interest rates and other earning opportunities do not exist.

Transfer pricing does exist. In earlier years it was a bitter bone of contention for less developed countries, who found that they had welcomed multinational firms to their shores but obtained very little tax revenue from their corporate profits. Eventually this led to a major United Nations investigation. More recently, it has begun to worry the United States government. There has been considerable foreign investment in the United States in the last decade but apparently these foreign multinationals are paying very little tax. The result is that the tax burden is thrown on to the shoulders of the domestic firms. This imposes a financial disadvantage on them in terms of their ability to raise capital for new developments etc., and eventually hampers their competitiveness.

Branch plants and regional problems

We have seen that the archetypal factory introduced by a multinational company is likely to take the form of a branch plant; a productive unit that produces commodities, often based upon the use of sub-components produced in other company plants, and possessing none of the decision-making functions of a home company. On the other hand governments seem eager to attract such plants.

One of the main reasons for this government enthusiasm lies in regional problems. In the United Kingdom there are considerable differences in unemployment and income levels between the northern and western areas of the country and the south and south east. Usually, one aim of government policies is to reduce these disparities (see H. Armstrong and J. Taylor, *Regional Economics*, Heinemann Educational, 1990). A key method to resolve the problem is to persuade companies to set up factories and offices in the poorer regions. By definition, a multinational company is mobile and looking for a site, and if the home economy is in a recession, multinational companies may be the sole source of such foot-loose firms. In addition, the executives of multinational firms may not share the subjective prejudices of domestic executives. For example, in the United Kingdom anywhere north of Watford may be viewed as a foreign country by a UK executive, whereas for decision-makers in a multinational anywhere in the United Kingdom is foreign, so Glasgow might be as good a location as Gloucester. Hence, multinational companies have played an important role in bringing new jobs into the less-developed areas of the United Kingdom.

The problem of such branch plants is that they are inherently unstable, as can be seen in the inset on Philips that follows. The decision-makers are elsewhere and the branch is merely a minor cog in a global framework. That framework may change with a change in product strategy, or a shift in exchange rates may dictate that that branch plant becomes uneconomic. Again, if the company is operating a transfer pricing strategy, a change in tax regimes elsewhere may lead to the closure of the UK plant. Similar possibilities apply to the branch plants of totally domestic companies, but there is a considerably greater probability of closure for the branch plant of a multinational firm. Hence, although regions welcome multinationals as a way of reducing unemployment, they live in fear of becoming a 'branch-plant' economy. In such a situation unemployment could rise rapidly owing to a series of decisions taken in far-off countries, and there is always the danger of the home economy stagnating, as new developments are placed overseas.

Philips cuts put British jobs at risk

by Derek Harris, Industrial Editor

Eight British factories with a workforce of 6000 are at risk in cuts, mainly among its European operations, ordered by Philips, the troubled Netherlands electronics conglomerate.

Philips said yesterday that it will plunge to losses of about 2 billion guilders (£651.5 million) this year against profits last year of 1.37 bn guilders as it radically restructures information systems, including computers, and components divisions.

In only a matter of weeks as profits have eroded, Philips has had to re-write the bill for restructuring from F1400 million to F12.7 billion to be set against 1990 profits.

The brunt of the 10,000 job losses out of a total workforce of nearly 300,000 world-wide will be taken by Continental Europe. It could be several months before the company makes detailed decisions on where the job cuts will fall.

Cutbacks in components manufacture would hit the British operations, which have a total workforce of just over 17,000. Electronic components, from semiconductors to television picture tubes, are manu-

factured by Philips in many countries round the world but the company is mainly concentrated in Europe.

Key British electronic components factories are at Blackburn (optical discs), Southport (television components) and Simonstown near Burnley (tube components), all in Lancashire, Durham (colour television tubes), Stockport, Cheshire (semiconductor devices), Southampton (design), Washington, Tyne and Wear (television components) and Dunfermline, Fife (printed circuit boards).

The bigger operations are Blackburn with Simonstown and Durham.

There are, though, some hopes at the British headquarters of Philips that its operations may not be as badly affected as in some other countries because measures to produce a fitter and leaner organization are already well advanced.

The British workforce has been reduced from about 23,000 over four years. This included the closure of a television assembly factory at Croydon, 18 months ago.

Source: *The Times*, 3 July 1990

The maintenance of competition

In essence the core of the competitive argument has been dealt with in the previous chapter. The entry of a multinational into a market may increase the competitive element in an industry in the short run. In the long run it might reduce it, as its overwhelming power allows it to take over or bankrupt the other firms in the industry. However, the relative importance of the problem for the domestic economy depends upon the effectiveness of the country's institutions for maintaining competition within markets. If there is a strong anti-trust legislation, that may suffice. However, there are dangers that, on the one hand, there could be a touch of xenophobia in its dealings with foreign multinationals, and on the other hand, a country could be so frightened of losing multinational investment that they would welcome it regardless. After all, if foreign firms are prevented from taking over domestic companies they might pull out altogether, and then become a strong supplier of competitive imports.

The abuse of power

It is certainly true that the size of many multinational firms, in financial terms, is greater than that of some small countries, especially less-developed countries. The expertise of their officials and officers may also exceed that of many government civil servants. These factors give them considerable advantages when negotiating with governments, other firms, or labour unions, and at times their strength may be used or misused. For example, by letting it be known that it is considering expansion in Europe, and that it is considering specific locations in five different countries, a company may exert implicit pressure on the relevant national governments or regional authorities to increase the level of grants and subsidies made available to it.

As indicated by the passage from *The Economist*, reproduced in the Data Response Question at the end of this chapter, the extent to which MNEs use or abuse their powers can only be guessed at. However, often such actions depend upon major differences in conditions between countries. Transfer pricing would lose its attraction if all countries taxed profits at similar rates. Playing one government off against another in order to gain advantageous investment grants would become less worthwhile if such grants were standardized across countries and regions. Much of the scope for the worst excesses of multinational firms could be reduced if there were greater cooperation and coordination between national governments.

Conclusion

The implication of the discussion above is that multinational firms probably do provide benefits for their host countries and such countries are right to welcome them. In particular, it is doubtful that any country, other than the supergiants, can hope to be equally efficient in all the activities that comprise a modern economy, and the growth of the multinationals is an important way of spreading advanced technology and products throughout the world. If they do bring problems to developed countries such problems are probably best dealt with by countries acting collectively to deal with them.

KEY WORDS

External costs and benefits	Branch plant
Cost – benefit analysis	Transfer pricing

Reading list

Armstrong, H. and Taylor, J., *Regional economics*, Heinemann Educational, 1990.

Bazen S. and Thirlwall, T., *Deindustrialization*, Heinemann Educational, 1989.

Bennett, P. and Cave, M., *Competition policy*, Heinemann Educational, 1991.

Eatwell, J., *Whatever Happened to Britain?*, chap. 3, Duckworth, 1983.

N.I.E.S.R., *The UK economy*, chaps 6 and 7, Heinemann Educational, 1990.

Paisley, R. and Quillfeldt, J., *Economics Investigated*, No.20: *Multinationals*, Collins, 1989.

Essay topics:

1. 'Reliance on multinational corporations brings short-run economic gains at the expense of long-run economic problems'. Discuss.
2. Are there any reasons why government attitudes to investment by foreign corporations should be viewed differently from their attitudes to investment by domestic companies?
3. Assess the costs and benefits of multinational firms to their home and host countries. (University of Oxford Delegacy of Local Examinations, 1990)
4. What are multinationals? What advantages do they enjoy over firms with a purely national base? (Oxford and Cambridge Examinations Syndicate, 1982).

Data Response Question 9
America's multinational blues
The article below, from *The Economist* of 21 July 1990, discusses how America is reacting to the new wave of foreign direct investment there. Read the passage and then answer the following questions.

1. Explain the terms 'transfer pricing', 'brass-plate companies', 'purchasing of influence', and 'technology transfer'.
2. Does the article evince any strong economic reasons for the supposed American dislike of multinational firms?
3. Critically evaluate the arguments in favour of multinational firms set out in the last two paragraphs of the article.

Opposition to foreign investment in the United States excites a strange feeling of déjà vu

Many Americans still find it hard to accept that they should be on the receiving end of that dread being, the 'multinational company'. Investing across borders or buying foreign companies are things that mighty American firms do to other people, or that foreigners may aspire to do to each other, but not things that foreigners should ever do to Americans. American firms did not invent the cross-border firm, but they so dominated its growth in the 1960s and 1970s that the words American and multinational became almost synonymous across the world, especially when muttered through gritted teeth. Now, just when many countries have learnt to tolerate this old public enemy number one, America is learning to hate it.

The latest multinational crime to be alleged in Washington is that of 'transfer pricing'. This is a trick whereby firms fiddle with the prices of goods bought from sister companies overseas in order to accumulate the most profit in countries where corporate taxes are lowest. Investigators for a committee of the House of Representatives report that 36 foreign-owned firms achieved a total of $329 billion in sales in 1977–87 but paid only $5 billion in American taxes.

Transfer pricing is a shabby practice wherever it happens and whoever is guilty of it; doubtless some foreign firms are doing it in America. But what is revealing is the way in which these American allegations are couched: the research singles out foreign-owned firms and compares them with domestic ones, rather than looking at all firms regardless of parentage. Remember that it was American firms that turned tax avoidance into an art form in the 1970s; then, as now, they used dodges aplenty to ship profits across borders, including America's whether by using brass-plate companies in the Caribbean or imaginative internal pricing, or other tricks. The target should be the practice, not the foreign practitioners.

The next storm will be another old American speciality: the purchasing of influence. This issue will rain down this autumn provided that a book by Mr. Pat Choate, a lobbyist at TRW, a high-tech firm, clears the libel lawyers. Mr. Choate will apparently chronicle how much Japanese firms spend on lobbying legislators in America, whom they hire, what victories they have won, and plenty of other Washington sleaze. Again, other countries who for years worried about rich American firms' clout will think this splendidly ironic. Here, as in much else, all the Japanese have done is follow a business maxim: do what the locals do, except better.

Up the learning curve

More noises will follow, all of a 1970s, Unctaddy(*) sort. There is already mumbling about technology transfer – either America is being deprived of it, or American technology is being stolen. Sovereignty (i.e. the loss of it) will pop up time and again. Such sentiments are matched by xenophobic fashions in American corporate advertising.

How can Americans learn to love their own business mimics? They would do well to remember why other countries (notably in Latin America) have gradually become happier to welcome the American multinationals they once feared. One reason is that free markets in capital and goods make bashing multinationals self-defeating; if you keep them out they'll only compete with you from somewhere else. Moreover, Latin American governments (after years of American preaching) now realise that direct investment is a much better way to receive foreign capital than loans. The money stays put, it is invested by experts, and the 'debt' will be serviced only to the extent that profit is made. Most of all, multinational investment by American firms in the 1970s was a boon for management skills and technology elsewhere. It exported American productivity worldwide. Now foreign inward investment is offering to do the same to America in areas where its skills are rusty. Nothing works such wonders as a dose of cultural imperialism.

* Explanatory note: UNCTAD stands for United Nations Conference on Trade, Aid and Development. This is an international organization concerned with the trade and development problems of less-developed countries.

Chapter Seven
Recent trends and future possibilities

'The "globalization" of business has been one of the great themes of the past decade, as more and more companies have rushed to expand across borders by making foreign acquisitions and mergers and investing in greenfield sites.' Guy de Jonquieres in the *Financial Times*, 4 April 1990

The story so far

Chapter 1 started with a quote from the Annual Report of a typical multinational firm, Foseco Plc, operating in 36 countries. In the interests of understanding the origins, operations, and associated problems of such firms, subsequent chapters tended to be couched within a limited framework. In considering why a firm expands abroad, and in which country it builds a factory or acquires another firm, etc., we concentrated on the specific decision by the firm, a specific advantage, and specific effects on the balance of payments. In so doing we rather played down the implications of the overall size of multinationals: the full range of products they may produce, or the large number of countries in which they may operate. However, size and diversity have become major characteristics of large multinationals in recent decades and it is these aspects that will dominate their actions, and governments' reactions to them, in the future.

Structures of large multinational firms

So far we have characterized the multinational firm as having a decision-making headquarters, located in a home country, linked directly to a variety of operations in many other countries. However, in the last two or three decades the largest multinationals have gone beyond that simple structure, in a number of ways.

The first development occurred in firms that, instead of simply making one-off decisions about expansion abroad, realized that they had arrived at a relatively full coverage of regional or world markets, and went on to plan their expansion from that wider perspective. Thus a chemical company, after expanding via a series of one-off decisions, may review the pattern of *worldwide* demand and then make location decisions in terms of how best to meet that demand. What is the optimum location pattern of plants to service the world market? Will it be necessary to set up a new plant in Malaysia, close down one in India, start production in West Africa, etc? The key factor is the switch from merely 'going multinational', to a consideration of *the world as the market*.

A second phenomenon has been the tendency of some manufacturing companies to *structure their operations* from a regional or world perspective. Instead of producing finished cars at six plants in six countries, the individual plants become specialized in the production of engines, gearboxes, body shells etc., and an *integrated network* of flows of components is set up between them. This situation is epitomized by the operations of the major car companies, such as Ford. For its operations in Europe, Ford considers the continent as the ground on which it is working, and its manufacturing operations are conceived on an integrated European scale. Engines are made at a restricted range of sites, such as Bridgend in South Wales, body shells are made elsewhere, and the components are all transferred to a third site for assembly. Other firms may follow a similar pattern but simply source the components they use on an international scale, rather than produce them within the firm. The extract on the Philips company given in the last chapter exhibited something of the same pattern, with television components made in various locations. It also indicated some of the national problems that might emerge when such a multinational company is forced into large-scale cutbacks overall. Rather than simply chopping off one or two plants, a change in company fortunes necessitates adjustments spread across the entire network of plants.

A further key element of recent decades has been that many multinational firms not only consider their own activities in continental or global terms, but they have also become keenly aware of the other producers in that world market. That is, there is now explicit recognition that, for many products, the regional, continental, or global market place is *oligopolistic* in nature. Firms' strategies are couched explicitly in terms of obtaining market power in regional, continental, or world terms. This trend may be observed in the business press every day. Discussion of major takeover bids or expansions is frequently set in a global context. One typical example of these trends is shown in the passage on Philip Morris.

The Philip Morris excerpt also illustrates another increasingly important factor. Many large multinational firms have become **conglomerates**. Note that although Philip Morris had other interests in coffee, it had very little activity in the confectionery market before the takeover. However, it had decided that confectionery was to be an important market on a global scale, and that it intended to enter that market. Many other multinationals, such as Unilever, are conglomerate in nature, and view the world in equally comprehensive terms.

Philip Morris to buy Suchard

William Dullforce in Geneva and Martin Dickson in New York

Philip Morris of the US, the world's biggest consumer products conglomerate, yesterday agreed to buy Switzerland's Jacobs Suchard, the world's third biggest chocolate and coffee group, for an estimated net cost of $3.8bn (£2.2bn).

The deal continues a world-wide struggle for the acquisition of brand names and market shares among the big global food groups.

It is the biggest takeover in the sector since Nestlé's £2.5bn acquisition of Britain's Rowntree in 1988, and will substantially enlarge the European position of Kraft General Foods, Philip Morris's food-processing arm.

It will give Philip Morris brand names such as Tobler, Toblerone, Mika, and Cote d'Or on the chocolate side and Night and Day, Jacques Vabre, Grand'Mere and Carte Noire in coffee.

Philip Morris said the deal gave it a big enough presence in Europe to compete against Nestlé and Unilever. The two coffee businesses would fit particularly well together since the US company, with brands such as Maxwell House, Hag and Kenco, was strong in Britain, Scandinavia and Spain, while Jacobs Suchard was a leading player in the French and German markets.

The takeover continues Philip Morris's rapid growth over the past six years into a leading food business, thus reducing its dependence on tobacco.

The deal will make it a significant player in the confectionery business, which it said was an 'emerging growth' area. It has little more than a chewing gum company in France and a baking chocolate business in the US.

Source: *Financial Times*, 19 June 1990.

Another recent phenomenon, resulting partly from the tendency of firms to view the world as their market, and to seek representation in all markets, has been the growth in **joint ventures** and strategic alliances, with possible consequences as indicated in the article on the following page.

The implications of these trends

There is nothing particularly new about the developments that we have just described; for example, firms have integrated their production on a national scale for years. Indeed, historically, one criticism of the British car industry was that it ferried around parts of cars from one factory in Birmingham to another, and transported car bodies from Oxford to Birmingham. Similarly, viewing a given geographical area as your market is common enough for firms of all sizes, and monopolies and oligopolies abound in many countries. Joint ventures by firms within the same country are not uncommon either, so why should we be concerned about these features in multinational firms?

Multinational links criticised

David Marsh in West Berlin

The growing number of strategic alliances between multinational companies was criticised yesterday as potential 'international cartels' by Mr. Wolfgang Kartte, president of the West German Federal Cartel Office.

Opening an international anti-trust conference in Berlin, he said such link-ups of 'champions' from the US, Japan and Europe could lead to a 'deformation of the world economy'.

He gave no examples, but is believed to have been thinking particularly of deals between Volkswagen and Ford in cars and Daimler and Mitsubishi in vehicles and engineering.

Mr. Kartte said the companies party to such alliances justified them on the grounds of seeking international partners in complementary areas. But there was a great danger of 'voluntary renunciation of competition', which could lead to private sector groups setting up their own market order.

Another criticism of big German companies was made by Mr. Otto Schlect, State Secretary in the Bonn Economics Ministry. He complained about calls in the car industry for controls on Japanese imports, and also took a side-swipe at last year's takeover by Daimler of the aerospace group Messerschmitt-Bolkow-Blohm.

Mr. Schlect said the increasing size of companies could lead to bureaucracy and lack of flexibility. He believed in 'the law of limited management resources' which restrained companies' abilities to operate across a large number of areas.

Source: *Financial Times*, 19 June 1990

First of all, it is quite possible that in taking these newer and global perspectives the multinational firm may have moved away from its original rationale. What is the 'specific advantage' of Nestlé, IBM, Hoechst, or Sony in the modern world? Such companies may have originated because of a particular technical expertise, or because of the development of some specific product, but this original advantage may no longer be valid. It may have been replaced by the advantages of brand names, managerial skill and sophistication, or technical excellence resulting from heavy expenditure on research and development. On the other hand, this may be equivalent to saying that the 'advantages' of such companies are now those of size and dominance, backed up by operating in oligopolistic concentrated industries across many countries. If one adds to this view the network of alliances and joint ventures that is being created between firms in different countries, the fear must be that eventually such companies will fall prey to the 'diseconomies' of large firms, particularly prevalent when they operate in controlled and oligopolistic markets. That is, they may become flabby, lose their competitive edge, and act as 'international cartels', to the detriment of consumer welfare.

The specific advantage hypothesis may explain the initial growth of multinationals but as they become large and dominant, the advantage may be overtaken by the **diseconomies** and less favourable welfare implications of large size (see Figure 5).

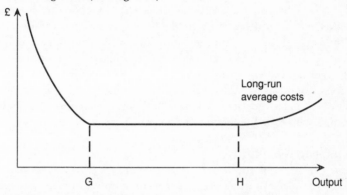

Figure 5 Diseconomies of scale

In the figure, over the output range GH the firm experiences constant returns to scale and produces at least cost. If the firm starts production with a very small output, and then increases the size of its production plants, it will experience economies of scale with decreasing average costs, until output level G is reached. However, if its size increases beyond H it will face diseconomies of scale, perhaps caused by the managerial difficulties involved in large organizations, and they will lead to rising costs.

Geographical Issues

Beyond these purely economic problems there are crucial geographical and political issues. In previous eras firms operated within one geographical area relating to one national or political entity. In the initial phase of expansion into multinational status the resulting problems were still only relevant to the individual country dealing with an individual multinational firm, without regard to the firm's activities in other markets or the situation of the other firms in the global market. Now the commonplace is that firms think and operate right across national and political boundaries. They work on an international, not a national, scale. But countries and their governments still operate on a national scale.

We have seen earlier, in the Philips example, some possible effects of this, where multinational decisions have implications across several countries. Further instances are provided by the problems currently facing the USA which is unilaterally trying to come to grips with the effects of transfer pricing. Almost certainly this problem requires international cooperation and coordination. Another example arises in the case of takeovers or mergers between firms based in different countries; for instance, the takeover of Rowntree Mackintosh by Nestlé was not referred to the UK Monopolies and Mergers Commission. Why should it be? Nestlé had only a small fraction of the UK chocolate market and the takeover did not lead to a marked increase in concentration in the UK industry. However, on the continent, and in individual continental countries, both Rowntree and Nestlé were important competitors, and the merger did increase concentration by a more marked amount. Thus, the home countries of the two firms may not have been affected, but the result of the takeover could well have been increased concentration in the French, German, or EC market as a whole.

The implied reaction

The key features of the above arguments are (i) there is less reason to believe that giant multinationals necessarily operate from any specific economic advantage, and more reason to believe that they may be players in an international oligopoly, and (ii) multinationals now frequently act and take decisions on a continental or global basis. In addition, there seems to be some, at present circumstantial, evidence, that global or regional concentration of industry is occurring.

The problems caused by these trends can only be resolved satisfactorily if individual countries cooperate and transcend their own boundaries. In mergers such as the Nestlé/Rowntree case, this would mean the European Community interfering as a matter of course, and regardless of whether one of the firms originates from outside the community. In the case of transfer pricing and the impact of taxes, there arises a clear need for international government agreement on the necessary legislation. Truly international firms necessitate an international response.

Wider issues

In the longer term one must expect that world National Income will increase, largely as a result of steady technological progress, and there will be continuing shifts in the patterns of consumer demands, demands for materials such as metals and minerals, and shifts in international economic power. Because of their international perspective MNEs will play a key role in the evolution of these trends.

However, two other factors will qualify their behaviour in future years. Firstly, there are the ramifications of political events such as the liberalization of Eastern Europe, the continued integration of the European Community in and after 1992, the continuing instability of the Gulf region and the change in the relative economic importance of major powers, such as the United States and Japan. Some of these may take the pressure away from present areas of the national interest/multinational firm friction, as firms take their expansionary fervour elsewhere, for example, into Eastern Europe. Others, such as continued extensive Japanese investment in the United States, may create additional problems.

Environmental concerns

The second major trend will be that of concern for the environment. As both individual consumers and national governments take action in the light of scientists' warnings this will imply quite rapid shifts in the pattern of demand from consumers, and the legislation applied to producers. A boost for organic foodstuffs, a shift towards catalytic converters for cars, a requirement to reduce energy demands, all could put pressure on multinational firms in particular.

Some indication of the importance of political and environmental features can be gleaned from the passage below, on the decision by Ford to switch investment in engine production away from Bridgend in South Wales to Cologne. Again, piecemeal government legislation by individual countries is likely to produce greater problems than would a coordinated approach. If individual countries adopt their own private standards, they will open up opportunities for their exploitation by multinational firms.

UK's push Europe's pull

Ford's decision to transfer the second stage of its planned investment to modernize its European engine manufacturing capacity from Bridgend to Cologne is a sign that the terms of competition for inward investment into Europe are changing. Labour relations in Ford UK plants have become more tense in the last three years and were a factor in the decision to move the £225m investment. But they were not the only one. The bulk of the UK programme will remain.

In the past decade, Ford has integrated its European manufacturing operations more closely than before. Just-in-time production techniques and single sourcing to cut costs make it much more vulnerable to industrial disruption. The unions, however, should not bear all the blame. Ford announced its Bridgend investment after the 1988 strike, which was much more costly than the recent dispute. In the mid-1980s Ford's senior executives probably over-estimated the extent to which industrial relations had changed in the UK. As a result, they planned to concentrate engine production in the UK. They are now backtracking from that judgement.

Improved relations

If not as good as one would like, labour relations are better than they used to be. Only on Friday, the Bridgend workforce accepted wide-ranging reforms in working practices to allow greater flexibility. Although the performance of the Dagenham plant is still a thorn in Ford's side, executives praise the productivity improvements which have been delivered at Halewood, once the bane of UK operations. Productivity in the British plants still lags behind those on the Continent, but in engines the gap is only 10 per cent. Once the UK's lower labour costs are taken into account, the difference in unit costs is negligible.

As Ford is shifting investment out of the UK, General Motors is investing £160m in an engine plant at Ellesmere, attracted by one of the most radical labour agreements yet signed in the industry. Ford itself has recently spent $1.6bn to acquire control of Jaguar.

The second factor in Ford's thinking was environmental concerns. As regulations start to tighten their grip on the industry, they will increasingly be reflected in investment plans. Ford has calculated that environmental controls mean the existing engine produced at Bridgend needs to have its life extended, while the single overhead camshaft engine produced at Cologne may now have a shorter life than expected a few years ago. Jobs and production should be maintained in Cologne by giving it some of the investment in the new range of lean-burn engines.

Industrial politics

Yet the third, and perhaps overwhelming, factor was the new industrial politics of Europe. When the investment plans for Bridgend were announced. IG Metall, the West German engineering union, joined forces with unions in Spain to complain of Ford's British bias. The prospect of German unification has created an even more powerful magnet for European industry. This is not the time to be seen retreating from the West German market, and unlike other car markers, Ford does not have joint-ventures in the east. In the mid-1980s, Bridgend may have looked like an attractive gateway to the post-1992 market. Now it looks a long way from Berlin.

Ford runs a large trade deficit on its UK operations. Only 61 per cent of its UK car sales last year were made up by products manufactured in Britain. The unions argue that it should match its sales in the UK, its largest European market, with a commitment to local manufacture. But as trade barriers crumble, the distinction between UK and European markets is going to become less relevant.

The rise in inward investment in the last few years still has considerable momentum. Japanese companies will continue to be attracted to the UK, and not only because of the Government's willingness to champion their cause as European companies. But that combative approach will have to take into account the fact that Bridgend is not the most accessible end of Europe.

Source: *Financial Times* 11 April, 1990

Conclusion

Multinational firms are here to stay for the foreseeable future at least. They will probably get bigger and more powerful, and they will probably continue to produce marked benefits for many people and many countries. On the other hand, their decisions may have increasingly marked effects on individuals and national governments. Many of the problems will probably best be resolved by governments acting in a coordinated and supranational way. If this does not occur there could be continual friction between the firms and national governments, leading to increased tension between the governments themselves.

KEY WORDS

Integrated network	Diseconomies
Conglomerates	Cartels
Joint ventures	

Reading list

Anderton, A.G., Work Card 44, 'The J. Car, G.M.'s Global Jigsaw' in *Data Response Workpack in A-Level Economics*, UTP, 1985.

Cook, M. and Healey, N., *Current Topics in International Economics*, Anforme, 1990 'MNEs, blessing or a curse?').

Davies, S. and Lund, M., 'MNEs: some issues and facts', *Economic Review*, March 1989.

Essay topics

1. Assess the strength of the argument for expecting the world to be dominated by a handful of multinational corporations in the year 2020.
2. Do multinational firms benefit the world economy?

Data Response Question 10

The passage that follows is taken from a review in the Financial Times of 9 April 1990 of Dr. DeAnne Julius' study *Global Companies and Public Policy* (Royal Institute of International Affairs, Pinter Publishers). Read the passage and answer the following questions.

1. Explain the terms 'Foreign Direct Investment', 'G-5 countries', 'international liberalization', 'regulatory structures', and 'protectionist pressures'.
2. Why would one expect differences in countries' growth rates to account for the pattern of FDI flows?
3. Explain in detail the argument about the distortionary effect of the conventional statistics of US foreign trade for 1986.
4. Why should 'weaker domestic producers' wish to introduce protectionist measures? What sort of arguments might they use?

Foreign investment 'changing structure of world economy'

Even today, the scale of Foreign Direct Investment (FDI) is almost certainly understated, since it is derived from national balance of payments statistics, which do not actually reflect foreign investments which are financed locally.

Furthermore, the study says, the true economic importance of FDI is reflected not in the value of assets of foreign-owned firms (FOFs), but in their sales. In the US, local sales by FOFs were one-and-a-half times bigger than the country's imports in 1985. FOFs in the US also account for more than half the country's exports and a third of its imports, while a further one fifth of imports are accounted for by shipments made by foreign subsidiaries of American-owned companies.

FDI growth is increasingly concentrated in the industrialized world, and flows to developing countries fell in real terms in the 1980s. Three quarters of the world's FDI stock is owned by the G-5 countries, though they account for only 42 per cent of world trade.

Dr. Julius says differentials in countries' growth rates do not explain the pattern of FDI flows. Though the business optimism generated by 1992 is acting as a stimulus in Europe, it is only one element in a wider global trend, she says.

She also believes trade protection has played only a small role in encouraging FDI. On the contrary, she concludes that the most important factor has been international liberalization, particularly of services – the sector where FDI has grown fastest in recent years.

'A crack has begun to open in the regulatory structures that have protected many service industries behind national borders. This crack is certain to open further' the study says.

Dr. Julius argues that these trends are robbing merchandise trade and balance of payments statistics of much of their meaning. A complete picture of international economic integration and countries' competitiveness can only be gained by taking account of sales and purchases by foreign-owned firms, since these effectively substitute for imports and exports. Re-calculating US trade figures to include transactions between American and foreign-owned companies, both in the US and abroad, the study estimates the country's total 'foreign sales' at $1,145bn and its 'foreign purchases' at $1,088bn in 1986.

On that basis, the US enjoyed a surplus on foreign sales of $57bn, compared with a $144bn merchandise trade deficit. Overall, the study finds the economic impact of FDI has been positive, and that foreign-owned companies do not behave much differently from domestic ones.

It argues that, as the economic contributions of foreign-owned firms are recognised, they will offset protectionist pressures from weaker domestic producers.

However, it emphasises that the full benefits of FDI will be realised only if governments treat foreign-owned and domestic firms equally and do not discriminate between trade and investment.

Source: Guy de Jonquieres, *Financial Times*, 9 April 1990.

Index